Cooking Activities A to Z

Join us on the web at

EarlyChildEd.delmar.com

Joanne Matricardi
Jeanne McLarty

THOMSON

DELMAR LEARNING

Australia Canada Mexico Singapore Spain United Kingdom United States

THOMSON

DELMAR LEARNING

Cooking Activities A to Z
Joanne Matricardi and Jeanne McLarty

Vice President, Career Education SBU:
Dawn Gerrain

Director of Editorial:
Sherry Gomoll

Acquisitions Editor:
Erin O'Connor

Editorial Assistant:
Stephanie Kelly

Director of Production:
Wendy A. Troeger

Production Manager:
JP Henkel

Production Editor:
Joy Kocsis

Production Assistant:
Angela Iula

Director of Marketing:
Wendy E. Mapstone

Channel Manager:
Kristin McNary

Marketing Coordinator:
David White

Cover Design:
Joseph Villanova

Composition:
Pre-Press Company, Inc.

Any additional questions about permissions can be submitted by email to thomsonrights@thomson.com

Library of Congress Cataloging-in-Publication Data

Matricardi, Joanne.
  Cooking activities A to Z / Joanne Matricardi and Jeanne McLarty.— 1st ed.
    p. cm. — (Activities A to Z series)
  Includes bibliographical references and index.
  ISBN 1-4018-7239-5
  1. Cookery—Study and teaching (Preschool)—Activity programs. 2. Early childhood education—Activity programs. I. McLarty, Jeanne. II. Title.
  TX661.M28 2005
  372.37'3—dc22   2005000021

NOTICE TO THE READER

Publisher does not warrant or guarantee any of the products described herein or perform any independent analysis in connection with any of the product information contained herein. Publisher does not assume, and expressly disclaims, any obligation to obtain and include information other than that provided to it by the manufacturer.

The reader is expressly warned to consider and adopt all safety precautions that might be indicated by the activities herein and to avoid all potential hazards. By following the instructions contained herein, the reader willingly assumes all risks in connection with such instructions.

The publisher makes no representation or warranties of any kind, including but not limited to, the warranties of fitness for particular purpose or merchantability, nor are any such representations implied with respect to the material set forth herein, and the publisher takes no responsibility with respect to such material. The publisher shall not be liable for any special, consequential, or exemplary damages resulting, in whole or part, from the readers' use of, or reliance upon, this material.

Contents

Preface

Cooking with preschoolers is an integral part of any early childhood nutrition program. Reports of childhood obesity are frequently in the news. This alarming trend has continued to scale upwards. Teaching children how to make good choices and limiting portions by preparing only individual recipes is one antidote to spiraling weight problems. The purpose of *Cooking Activities A to Z* is to provide teachers, families, and student teachers with a collection of hands-on activities enabling the young child to experience cooking procedures. Most of the recipes give children practice in making an individual portion. Portion control and allowing children to serve themselves are two methods of combating obesity (Squires, 2004). Adults have a tendency to put too much food on a child's plate; a child's portion is typically half that of an adult. One way to measure a portion correctly is to give the child 1 tablespoon of food per year of age (Herr, 2002). For example, a three-year-old would have three tablespoons of peas, three tablespoons of rice, and so on.

Cooking Activities A to Z presents recipes in an alphabetical layout. This allows adults to link a cooking curriculum to specific letters of the alphabet. Many preschool classrooms focus on a letter of the week. This book provides an easy way for cooking activities to highlight a particular letter.

The activities are presented in a lesson plan format with five main areas: "Developmental Goals," "Learning Objective," "Materials," "Adult Preparation," and "Procedures." The developmental goals offer cooking concepts as well as physical and social considerations. The learning objective states what the children will use to accomplish the immediate goal of the lesson. The materials section presents all that is required to complete the lesson, from preparation through implementation of the activity. The "Procedures" section involves a step-by-step process for the child to successfully accomplish the lesson.

Additional sections may be included in the lesson plan format. Safety precautions are presented when objects used by children may necessitate a need for closer supervision. The use of heat or small foods that may present a choking hazard are examples of situations that require additional care.

A "Notes" section may be present if there are explanations of different outcomes or allergy considerations. Adults need to be aware of children's health concerns. A growing number of children have food allergies. Reactions to peanuts or other nuts are more common. When nuts are used, substitutions are suggested. Milk allergies are also being seen more frequently. Rice or soy milk and vegetable "cheese" products may be substituted for dairy products. Most of the recipes are written for an individual child, so the substitutions do not need to affect the entire class. Parents are usually very amenable to providing the ingredients for variations for their child. But once again, be aware of each child's individual needs. Some children are so highly allergic to peanut butter that they may have a reaction, without touching it, by merely being present in a room where it is being used.

A growing number of preschool children are vegetarian. Vegetarian substitutions are therefore provided following recipes in which meat products are used. The parents of vegetarian children are usually happy to supply the needed soy alternatives.

Age appropriateness for activities is given. These are just suggestions. Knowing the children's abilities and attention span will help determine what activities may be done and whether or not they need to be altered. As much as possible, these activities are written to allow children to create their own food from start to finish, so the lessons may be used with individual children, with small groups, or with the entire class.

A suggested group size is also given for each activity. Traditionally, when cooking, the number of children involved equals the age of the children. Therefore, when cooking with two-year-olds, two children participate at one time; with three-year-olds, three children may cook with one adult, and so on. When introducing a new form of cooking, using more advanced measurements, or using heat, it is best to keep the ratio of children to adults as small as possible. As children become more adept, additional children may be included in the procedures.

Teachers need to be aware of their centers' policies concerning the use of cooking appliances. Some schools permit the use of hot plates or electric skillets; other schools will not allow these electrical appliances in the classroom. You can easily adapt recipes that call for cooking in the classroom by having the children measure and mix the ingredients and then taking the mixtures into the kitchen for the actual cooking.

Teachers also need to follow their schools' policies regarding the use of sugar. Some of the recipes require that sugar be added or that a product containing sugar, such as pudding, be used. Limit the amount of sugar a child eats. It is our belief that if sweets are totally withheld, children may binge on these items when they are allowed to make their own choices. Children should be taught to eat items with sugar infrequently and in small portions.

Appendixes that follow the activities give charts of measurement equivalents. These will enable the adult to adapt favorite recipes for fewer children by dividing the amounts needed into smaller measurements. Recipes may also be increased to accommodate larger groups or families.

Last, *Cooking Activities A to Z* provides an "Index of Units." This allows the adult to match cooking activities to a theme-based curriculum. Whether activities are chosen to facilitate a unit or highlight an alphabet letter, the key is to promote cooking for young children. Cooking enhances self-esteem, promotes independence, and provides nutritious experiences.

ONLINE COMPANION™

An Online Companion™ is an accompaniment to *Cooking Activities A to Z*. This site contains additional hands-on cooking activities for young children. The activities are written in the same lesson plan format that is found in this book. These detailed plans include developmental goals, learning objectives, a list of materials, directions for adult preparation, and a step-by-step procedure for the child. The activities are creative, easy to understand, and simple to implement, either in the preschool classroom or at home.

The *Cooking Activites A to Z* Online Companion™ also provides links to helpful Web sites. Please visit http://www.earlychilded.delmar.com to gain access to this Online Companion™.

ACKNOWLEDGMENTS

This book is an accumulation of original and shared ideas developed over 40 years of teaching young children. Many thanks to our coworkers, students, and their parents for sharing and experimenting with us. We would also like to express our appreciation to Alice Volz and Gloria Matricardi for sharing the family recipes and to Anna, Cara, Danielle, and Carl Matricardi for enduring many years of experimental cooking as the recipes were perfected.

We, and the editors at Thomson Delmar Learning, would also like to thank the following reviewers for their time, effort, and thoughtful contributions which helped to the shape the final text:

Wendy Bertoli
Early Childhood Instructor
Lancaster County Career and Technical
Center, PA

Cheryl Cranston
Early Childhood Educator
Hope Springs Child Care Center, OR

Heather Fay
Child Care Consultant
Akron, OH

Vicki Folds, Ed.D.
Early Childhood Instructor
Broward Community College, FL

Jody Martin
Education and Training Coordinator
Crème de la Crème Child Care Centers, CO

Brenda Schin
Early Childhood Consultant
Ballston Spa, NY

Joanne Matricardi
Jeanne McLarty

HELPFUL HINTS

Throughout the years, we've developed strategies that help our cooking activities to proceed more efficiently. The following helpful hints are routinely used in our classrooms.

✄ The adult needs to read the recipe through to make sure all ingredients and equipment are ready.

✄ Do all the adult preparation ahead of time to help the cooking experience move smoothly.

✄ Baking times may vary according to the oven and the quantity that is being cooked at one time.

✄ Using muffin liners creates child-size portions. Foil muffin liners are preferred to paper liners. Foil liners are sturdier and allow the child to add multiple ingredients directly into the liner. Foil liners may be placed directly onto a baking sheet. Muffin tins may be used but are not mandatory. This allows the adult to bake more servings than a muffin tin would allow.

✄ Identify the items the child has made by lining the baking sheets with aluminum foil; write children's names with permanent marker to identify what each child made. When using the foil muffin liners, write the child's name on the bottom of the liner.

✄ Preschoolers may measure their own ingredients. To facilitate this, put the ingredients in bowls for children to dip measuring spoons into.

✄ Using nesting measuring cups makes it easier for a child to measure than using a larger measuring cup and trying to level the ingredients to match a specific mark.

✄ When using measuring spoons, preschoolers may need to use a small spoon, craft stick, or plastic knife to remove sticky ingredients from the spoon.

✄ Cooking in the classroom may be done by using hot plates or electric skillets, with close adult supervision. Electric skillets are preferred, because the hot plate with a pan on it is higher than the electric skillet.

✄ Cooking with an electric skillet also works well at home. The child can see better at the table as opposed to standing on a chair or step stool at the stove.

✄ If possible, use child-size tables and chairs.

✂ When working with children under age 3, the adult may measure and the children may pour and mix.

✂ Rinse additional fat from ground beef by placing the meat in a colander and rinsing it with running water.

SAFETY PRECAUTIONS

Cooking requires additional safety precautions. The following practices are standard in our classrooms:

✂ Wash all fruits and vegetables thoroughly with running water. *Vegetarian Times* cautions against using soap because produce will absorb the soap (Hise, 2004).

✂ When using a hot plate or electric skillet, roll towels and place around the appliance to create a buffer between the heat and the child.

✂ If the adult needs to leave the room, lift the electric appliance out of reach. Make sure the cord is also out of reach.

✂ Do not leave a cord plugged into an outlet once the appliance has been detached. This is like leaving an outlet uncovered.

✂ If using equipment with a cord, tape the cord to the table and floor. This is to ensure the appliance doesn't get pulled off the table by a dangling cord and also prevents people from tripping over a cord on the floor.

✂ Always supervise children closely when cooking. Small foods may present a choking hazard in young children.

EQUIPMENT AND SUPPLIES

This equipment and supply list contains items to keep on hand. It does not include the food items that will need to be purchased for each activity. Standard equipment may be purchased at discount stores or garage sales. Families may also be asked to donate items for cooking projects (see "Cooking Wish List and Family Letter" and "Activity-Specific Family Letter").

3-ounce cups	Cups	Measuring cups— plastic, nesting	Resealable plastic bags
5-ounce cups	Custard cups	Melon baller	Salt shaker (empty)
10-ounce clear plastic cup	Cutting board	Microwave	Saucepan
9" x 13" cake pan	Egg beater	Mixing bowl	Small ice cream scoop
Aluminum foil	Electric mixer	Muffin tin	Smocks
Apple corer	Electric skillet (non-stick)	Nut chopper	Spatula
Baking sheets	Foil muffin liners	Oven	Spoons—metal
Blender	Forks	Pan	Spoons—wooden
Bowls (small)	Funnel	Paper plates	Star cookie cutters
Can opener (smooth edge)	Globe	Paper towels	Stove
Child-size pitcher	Grater	Pastry brush	Timer
Child-size rolling pin	Heart-shaped cookie cutter	Permanent marker	Tongs
Child-size scissors	Hot plate	Plastic bowls—large and small	Toothpicks
Chopsticks	Kitchen scissors	Plastic cups with lids	Towels
Colander	Knives	Plastic knives	Trays
Cooking pot	Masking tape	Plastic wrap	Vegetable peeler
Cotton towel (small)	Measuring cups— glass	Plates	Wax paper
Crock pot		Refrigerator	Wooden skewers

COOKING WISH LIST AND FAMILY LETTER

Dear Family,

We are in need of several items for our cooking activities. If you are able to donate any of the circled items below, please notify your child's teacher.

9" x 13" cake pan	Muffin tin
Apple corer	Nut chopper
Baking sheets	Pan
Blender	Plastic cups with lids
Can opener (smooth edge)	Plastic knives
Chopsticks	Plastic wrap
Cloth	Plates
Colander	Salt shaker (empty)
Custard cups	Saucepan
Cutting board	Small ice cream scoop
Egg beater	Spatula
Electric mixer	Spoons—metal
Grater	Spoons—wooden
Measuring cups—glass	Star cookie cutters
Measuring cups—plastic, nesting	Timer
Melon baller	Tongs
Microwave	Trays
Mixing bowl	Vegetable peeler

ACTIVITY-SPECIFIC FAMILY LETTER

Dear Family,

We will do the following cooking activity on _____.
Please send in the requested ingredient on this day.
Cooking Activity: _____
Ingredient: _____

Thank you,

Ambrosia

AGES: 2–5

DEVELOPMENTAL GOALS:

✂ To practice measuring

✂ To develop eye-hand coordination

LEARNING OBJECTIVE:

The child will measure fruit and place fruit into a bowl to make ambrosia.

MATERIALS:

Ingredients	Equipment
Bananas	Knife
Mandarin oranges	Cutting board
Seedless grapes	Bowls
Peaches	Measuring spoons
Lemon juice	Measuring cups
Water	Can opener
Shredded coconut	

ADULT PREPARATION:

1. Cut banana into small pieces.
2. Soak the banana in a mixture of 1–2 tablespoons of lemon juice and 1 cup of water to prevent it from turning brown.

continued

Ambrosia continued

3. Cut the seedless grapes in half lengthwise, and place them in a bowl.

4. Purchase diced peaches or cut whole peaches into small pieces, and place them in a bowl.

5. Place the shredded coconut in a bowl.

6. Open the can of mandarin oranges and drain the juice. Place the mandarin oranges in a bowl.

7. Drain the lemon mixture off the bananas, and place them in a bowl.

PROCEDURES:

The child will complete the following steps:

1. Wash hands.

2. Measure ⅛ cup (2 tablespoons) of each fruit, and place the fruit in a bowl.

3. Sprinkle the fruit with shredded coconut.

Note: If any children have an allergy to coconut, delete this ingredient.

SAFETY PRECAUTION:

Supervise children closely when working with small foods such as grapes to prevent choking.

GROUP SIZE:

2–5 children

Apple Treats

AGES: 2½–5

DEVELOPMENTAL GOALS:

✂ To experience joy in cooking

✂ To follow directions

LEARNING OBJECTIVE:

The child will follow directions to make apple treats.

MATERIALS:

Ingredients	Equipment
Apples	Resealable plastic bags
Cinnamon	Apple corer
Sugar	Measuring spoons
Lemon juice	Paper plates
Water	Bowls

ADULT PREPARATION:

1. Wash one apple each for two children.

2. Core and slice ½ apple per child.

3. Measure 1–2 tablespoons of lemon juice and 1 cup of water into a bowl. Add the apple slices to the mixture to prevent them from turning brown.

continued

Apple Treats continued

4. When ready to move all ingredients to the table, drain the lemon mixture off the apples.

5. Place apple slices on a paper plate for each child.

6. Pour cinnamon and sugar in separate bowls.

7. Place ingredients and supplies on the table.

PROCEDURES:

The child will complete the following steps:

1. Wash hands.

2. Open the resealable bag.

3. Measure 1 teaspoon of sugar and place it in the bag.

4. Measure 1 teaspoon of cinnamon and place it in the bag.

5. Seal the bag, with adult assistance if needed.

6. Shake the bag until the cinnamon and sugar are mixed.

7. Reopen the bag.

8. Put apple slices in the bag.

9. Seal the bag; shake and move the bag around, covering the apples with the cinnamon and sugar mixture.

10. Open the bag; place the apple treats on a plate to eat for snack.

GROUP SIZE:

2–4 children

Awesome Apple Cobbler

AGES: 3–5

DEVELOPMENTAL GOALS:

✂ To promote measurement skills

✂ To follow a sequence

LEARNING OBJECTIVE:

The child will measure and sequence ingredients to create an individual cobbler.

MATERIALS:

Ingredients	Equipment
Box of yellow cake mix Softened margarine 21-ounce can of apple pie filling (serves 10–12)	Foil muffin liners Permanent marker Baking sheet or muffin tin Can opener Measuring spoons Bowls Resealable plastic bag Knife

continued

5

Awesome Apple Cobbler continued

ADULT PREPARATION:

1. Preheat oven to 350°.
2. Open can of pie filling and pour contents into a bowl.
3. Cut the apples in the pie filling into smaller pieces.
4. Pour ¼ to ½ of the cake mix into another bowl.
5. Store the remaining cake mix in a resealable plastic bag.
6. Write each child's name on an individual muffin liner.

PROCEDURES:

The child will complete the following steps:

1. Wash hands.
2. Select the foil muffin liner with his or her name.
3. Measure 2 tablespoons of apple pie filling and put it in the liner.
4. Measure 1 tablespoon of cake mix and sprinkle it over the top of the apples.
5. Measure 1 teaspoon of softened margarine and place it in the center of the muffin liner.
6. Place the cobbler onto the baking sheet or muffin tin, with adult assistance if necessary.

When the baking sheet or muffin tray is full, the adult will bake the awesome apple cobblers for 25–30 minutes or until the topping is golden brown.

GROUP SIZE:

3–5 children

Banana Muffins

AGES: 3–5

DEVELOPMENTAL GOALS:

- ✂ To observe a transformation
- ✂ To promote nutrition

LEARNING OBJECTIVE:

The child will take part in observing a transformation of the ingredients into a nutritious snack.

MATERIALS:

Ingredients	Equipment
Softened butter or margarine Sugar Egg substitute Ripe bananas Self-rising flour	Bowls Plate Measuring spoons Muffin tin Foil muffin liners Permanent marker Fork

ADULT PREPARATION:

1. Place flour, sugar, egg substitute, and softened butter or margarine in bowls.

2. Slice ripe banana into approximately 2" slices.

3. Place the banana slices on a plate.

continued

Banana Muffins continued

4. Write each child's name on the bottom of a foil muffin liner.
5. Preheat the oven to 350°.
6. Set a bowl on the table for each child.

PROCEDURES:

The child will complete the following steps:

1. Wash hands.
2. Place a banana slice in a bowl.
3. Mash the banana with a fork.
4. Measure 1 teaspoon of butter or margarine and add it to the bowl.
5. Measure 1 teaspoon of egg substitute and pour it into the bowl.
6. Stir the ingredients with the fork.
7. Measure 2 teaspoons of sugar and add it to the bowl.
8. Measure 2 tablespoons and 2 teaspoons of self-rising flour.
9. Add the flour to the bowl and stir all the ingredients with a fork, mixing well.
10. Spoon the banana mixture into the muffin liner that has his or her name on the bottom, with adult help if necessary.

The adult will complete the following steps:

1. Place the liner in the muffin tin.
2. Once the muffin tin is full, bake the muffins for approximately 25 minutes or until golden brown.

GROUP SIZE:

3–5 children

Bear Paws

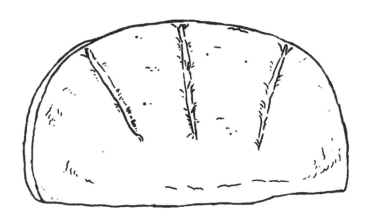

MATERIALS:

Ingredients	Equipment
Canned biscuit dough Shredded cheddar cheese	Baking sheet Spoon Aluminum foil Permanent marker Plastic knife Paper plates Bowl

ADULT PREPARATION:

1. Preheat oven to 350°.
2. Cover baking sheet with aluminum foil.
3. Open the can of biscuits and place each one on a separate paper plate.
4. Place the shredded cheese in a bowl.

PROCEDURES:

The child will complete the following steps:

1. Wash hands.
2. Select a plate with the biscuit dough.
3. Place the flat part of the hand on the biscuit dough; press down to flatten.

continued

AGES: 2–5

DEVELOPMENTAL GOALS:

✄ To help develop fine motor skills

✄ To participate in a cooking activity

LEARNING OBJECTIVE:

The child will cut with a knife to enhance fine motor skills while participating in cooking bear paws.

Bear Paws continued

4. Spoon shredded cheese in the center of the flattened biscuit.

5. Fold the biscuit in half.

6. Press down around the edges, making a seal, with adult help if necessary.

7. Use the plastic knife and cut three slits in the dough to resemble a paw print.

The adult will complete the following steps:

1. Place the bear paw on the foil-covered cookie sheet.

2. Write the child's name below the dough.

3. Place bear paws approximately two inches apart on the baking sheet.

4. When the baking sheet is full, place the dough in the oven and bake for 12–15 minutes until the biscuit is golden brown.

GROUP SIZE:

2–5 children

Broccoli Salad

AGES: 3–5

DEVELOPMENTAL GOALS:

✂ To follow directions

✂ To promote small muscle development

LEARNING OBJECTIVE:

The child will use small muscles while following directions to add and mix ingredients to make broccoli salad.

MATERIALS:

Ingredients	Equipment
Fresh broccoli florets	Nut chopper
Raisins	Cutting board
Mayonnaise	Measuring spoons
Sugar	¼-cup measure
	Spoon
	5-ounce cup
	Permanent marker
	Tray

continued

Broccoli Salad continued

ADULT PREPARATION:

1. Place broccoli, raisins, mayonnaise, and sugar in separate bowls.
2. Place bowls, nut chopper, cutting board, spoons, and cups on the table.
3. Using a permanent marker, write children's names on individual cups.

PROCEDURES:

The child will complete the following steps:

1. Wash hands.
2. Measure 1 teaspoon of mayonnaise and place it in the 5-ounce cup.
3. Measure ¼ teaspoon of sugar and place it in the cup.
4. Stir the mixture well.
5. Select a broccoli floret and place it on the cutting board.
6. Position the chopper over the broccoli, with adult help if needed.
7. Cut the broccoli into pieces using the pump action of the chopper.
8. Measure the broccoli that has been chopped (¼ cup of broccoli is needed).
9. Place ¼ cup of chopped broccoli in the 5-ounce cup.
10. Add 1 teaspoon of raisins to the cup.
11. Stir the mixture until the broccoli and raisins are coated with the sweet mayonnaise.

The adult will complete the following steps:

1. Place the child's cup on the tray.
2. Refrigerate the tray of broccoli salad cups until snack or lunch time.

SAFETY PRECAUTION:

Supervise children closely when using small foods such as raisins to prevent choking.

GROUP SIZE:

3–5 children

Chicken Pot Pie

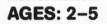

DEVELOPMENTAL GOALS:

- ✂ To practice measuring
- ✂ To properly sequence ingredients

LEARNING OBJECTIVE:

The child will practice sequencing and measuring ingredients to make chicken pot pie.

MATERIALS:

Ingredients	Equipment
Chicken	Pot for boiling chicken
Water	Knife
Frozen mixed vegetables	Bowls
Cream of celery soup	Measuring spoons
(10¾-ounce can—	Measuring cup
by weight—equals 1 cup—	Foil muffin liners
by volume)	Permanent marker
Self-rising flour	Muffin pan
Milk	Fork for mixing flour
Spray margarine (found in	and milk
dairy aisle of grocery store)	

ADULT PREPARATION:

1. Clean the chicken with cold running water.
2. Put enough water in a pot to cover the chicken.
3. Boil the chicken on the stove. A whole chicken takes almost one hour.
4. Cool the chicken and cut it into child-size pieces.

continued

Chicken Pot Pie continued

5. Put chicken in a bowl.

6. Pour cream of celery soup in a separate bowl.

7. Mix the soup with ½ cup of water.

8. Mix ¾ cup of milk with ¾ cup of self-rising flour.

9. Thaw vegetables in the microwave and place in a bowl.

10. Write children's names on the bottoms of individual muffin liners, with a permanent marker.

11. Preheat the oven to 350°.

12. Set spray margarine and bowls of chicken, soup, vegetables, and flour-milk mixture on the table.

13. Set the measuring spoons, liners, and muffin tin on the table.

PROCEDURES:

The child will complete the following steps:

1. Wash hands.

2. Find the liner with his or her name written on the bottom.

3. Measure the following ingredients and layer them in the muffin liner in the following order:

   a. 1 tablespoon of chicken

   b. 1 tablespoon of vegetables

   c. 1 teaspoon of soup

   d. 1 tablespoon of the flour-milk mixture

4. Squirt the top of the flour mixture with spray margarine.

The adult will complete the following steps:

1. Help the child place the liner in the muffin tin.

2. When the muffin tin is full, place the mini chicken pot pies in the oven for 30–40 minutes or until the topping is golden brown.

Note: Canned chicken, packed in water, may be used instead of boiled chicken.

VEGETARIAN SUBSTITUTION:

Use small pieces of firm tofu in place of chicken.

GROUP SIZE:

2–5 children

Chicken Salad

AGES: 3–5

DEVELOPMENTAL GOALS:

✂ To introduce nutritious foods

✂ To enhance eye-hand coordination

LEARNING OBJECTIVE:

Using eye-hand coordination, the child will measure and mix ingredients to make a nutritious chicken salad.

MATERIALS:

Ingredients	Equipment
Chicken	Pot to boil chicken
Water	Knife
Celery	Bowls
8-ounce container of cream cheese, softened	Spoons
Red grapes	Measuring spoons
	Masking tape
	Permanent marker

ADULT PREPARATION:

1. Rinse chicken with cool, running water.
2. Boil the chicken and cut it into child-size pieces.
3. Chop celery into small pieces.
4. Cut grapes in half, lengthwise.

continued

Chicken Salad continued

5. Put chicken, celery, and grapes into separate bowls.

6. Place the softened tub of cream cheese, the bowls of food, a spoon, and an empty bowl (for the child to mix ingredients in) on the table.

PROCEDURES:

The child will complete the following steps:

1. Wash hands.

2. Measure 2 tablespoons of chicken into the bowl.

3. Measure 1 teaspoon of cream cheese and mix it with the chicken.

4. Measure and add a tablespoon of grapes and a tablespoon of celery to the chicken.

5. Mix all ingredients together.

The adult will complete the following steps:

1. Write child's name on masking tape and place it on the bowl.

2. Refrigerate the chicken salad to eat at lunch or snack time. May be served with crackers, bread, or on a bed of lettuce.

SUBSTITUTION:

Tuna may be substituted for chicken.

VEGETARIAN SUBSTITUTION:

Firm tofu may be used in place of chicken.

SAFETY PRECAUTION:

Supervise children closely when small foods such as grapes are used, to prevent choking.

GROUP SIZE:

2–5 children

Chili

AGES: 3–5

DEVELOPMENTAL GOALS:

✄ To practice self-help skills

✄ To enjoy a nutritious snack

LEARNING OBJECTIVE:

The child will measure and mix ingredients to make chili.

MATERIALS:

Ingredients	Equipment
16-ounce can of chili beans with mild sauce (16-ounce can equals 1¾ cups, which equals 28 tablespoons) 15-ounce can of tomato sauce (27 tablespoons) Small onion ½ pound ground beef ½ pound of ground sausage	Food chopper Skillet Spoon Colander Plate Paper towels Can opener Bowls Measuring spoons Foil muffin liners Muffin baking tin Permanent marker

ADULT PREPARATION:

1. Chop onion.
2. Brown ground beef and sausage with onion, stirring as needed.

continued

Chili continued

3. Drain the grease from the beef-sausage mixture, using a colander. After draining, the mixture should equal approximately 38 tablespoons.

4. Layer a plate with paper towels.

5. Put the meat and onions on the plate with towels.

6. Open the cans of tomato sauce and chili beans.

7. Put the sauce and beans in separate bowls.

8. Set the meat, sauce, and beans on the table.

9. Write the children's names on the bottoms of the muffin liners.

10. Preheat the oven to 350°.

PROCEDURES:

The child will complete the following steps:

1. Wash hands.

2. Measure and place the following ingredients in a bowl:

   a. 2 tablespoons of meat and onion mixture

   b. 1 tablespoon plus 1 teaspoon of tomato sauce

   c. 1–2 tablespoons of beans

3. Stir the ingredients well and then place them in the foil muffin liner bearing his or her name.

The adult will complete the following steps:

1. Place the child's muffin liner in a muffin tin.

2. When the muffin tray is full, bake the chili at 350° for 10 minutes.

3. Serve with crackers.

Note: Shredded cheese may be sprinkled on top of the chili.

VEGETARIAN SUBSTITUTION:

Use crumbled meatless ground burger. It is found in the frozen foods part of the grocery store and is precooked and ready to use. Vegetarian servings may need to be cooked in a separate muffin pan. At times the juices may overflow.

GROUP SIZE:

2–5 children

Dinosaur Eggs

D

AGES: 2–5

DEVELOPMENTAL GOALS:

- ✄ To increase fine motor skills
- ✄ To observe transformations

LEARNING OBJECTIVE:

The child will develop fine motor and observation skills in making dinosaur eggs.

MATERIALS:

Ingredients	Equipment
Red, purple, or blue powdered drink mix (unsweetened) Water Eggs	Child-size pitcher Saucepan Small clear cups Tray Masking tape Permanent marker Resealable plastic bags

ADULT PREPARATION:

1. Put eggs into a saucepan.
2. Cover with water.
3. Heat eggs until the water boils.
4. Boil for three minutes.
5. Remove eggs and let cool.

continued

Dinosaur Eggs continued

6. Mix the powdered drink mix in a pitcher with the amount of water the package requires. Do not add sugar. (Dark colors such as purple, blue, or red work best.)

7. Pour the drink mix in a child-size pitcher.

PROCEDURES (DAY 1):

The child will complete the following steps:

1. Wash hands.

2. Roll an egg on a table, exerting pressure with the hand and causing the shell to crack all over. (Shell should not be removed.)

3. Put the egg into a clear cup.

4. Using the child-size pitcher, cover the egg with drink mix.

The adult will complete the following steps:

1. Write the child's name on a piece of masking tape with a permanent marker and place the tape on the child's cup.

2. Put each child's cup on one tray.

3. Set the tray in the refrigerator. Leave the eggs, soaking in the drink mix, overnight.

PROCEDURES (DAY 2):

The child will complete the following steps:

1. Wash hands.

2. Watch as the adult drains the drink mix off the eggs and discards the drink mix.

3. Peel the shell off the egg and discard the egg shells, with adult help if necessary. The drink mix will have soaked through the cracks in the shell, staining the boiled egg.

4. Eat the egg for a snack or put it in a resealable plastic bag to take home.

Note: Let parents know if the egg is placed in the child's book bag.

SAFETY PRECAUTIONS:

If eggs were not refrigerated, do not eat them. Always wash your hands and have the children wash their hands after handling eggs.

GROUP SIZE:

2–4 children

Dirt and Worms

AGES: 2½–5

DEVELOPMENTAL GOALS:

- ✂ To experience joy in cooking
- ✂ To develop rational counting skills

LEARNING OBJECTIVE:

The child will experience joy in cooking and practice rational counting while making a fun dessert.

MATERIALS:

Ingredients	Equipment
Instant chocolate pudding mix Milk Chocolate sandwich cookies Edible candy worms	Large bowl Mixing spoon Resealable plastic bags Plate Child-size rolling pins Clear, plastic 10-ounce cups Permanent marker Tray

ADULT PREPARATION:

1. Mix instant pudding with milk in a large bowl, according to the package directions.
2. Refrigerate pudding according to package directions.

continued

21

Dirt and Worms continued

3. Place two sandwich cookies in a resealable plastic bag for each child.
4. Set worms in a bowl.
5. Write each child's name on a clear plastic cup.
6. When pudding is set, place pudding, worms, bagged cookies, cups, rolling pins, and spoons on the table.

PROCEDURES:

The child will complete the following steps:

1. Wash hands.
2. Measure ⅓ cup of pudding and put it in the clear plastic cup bearing his or her name.
3. Use a rolling pin to roll over the cookies in the baggie, continue rolling until the cookies are crushed.
4. Pour the crumbs out of the baggie and onto the pudding in a cup.
5. Count out two candy worms.
6. Place the candy worms in the pudding cup.
7. Place the cup on a tray.

The adult will complete the following step:

1. Refrigerate the tray of dirt and worm cups until snack time.

Note: If child-size rolling pins are not available, small cups may be rolled over the cookies.

⚠ SAFETY PRECAUTION:

Supervise children closely when using candy worms, because they present a choking hazard.

GROUP SIZE:

2–5 children

Double-Baked Potatoes

AGES: 4–5

DEVELOPMENTAL GOALS:

✁ To participate in a cooking activity

✁ To make healthy snacks

LEARNING OBJECTIVE:

The child will participate in making a healthy double-baked potato.

MATERIALS:

Ingredients	Equipment
Potatoes Milk Softened butter or margarine Shredded cheddar cheese	Fork Knife Baking sheet Aluminum foil Permanent marker Melon baller Spoons Measuring spoons Bowls

continued

Double-Baked Potatoes continued

ADULT PREPARATION:

1. Preheat the oven to 350°.
2. Wash potatoes. Use one potato for two children.
3. Using a fork, poke holes in the potatoes.
4. Bake the potatoes for approximately one hour, or until they are tender when pierced with a fork.
5. Cut the potatoes in half, lengthwise, and set them aside to cool.
6. Cover a baking sheet with aluminum foil.
7. Put milk, butter, and shredded cheese into separate bowls.
8. Set all ingredients on the table.

PROCEDURES:

The child will complete the following steps:

1. Wash hands.
2. Scoop the potato out of the skin using a melon baller, with adult help if necessary. Try to keep the skin intact.
3. Place the scooped potato in a bowl.
4. Measure the following ingredients and place them in the bowl with the potato:

    a. 2 teaspoons milk

    b. ½ teaspoon butter or margarine

    c. 1 tablespoon shredded cheese

5. Mix the ingredients well with a fork.
6. Place the potato mixture back in the potato skin, with adult help if necessary.
7. Place the potato on the foil-covered baking sheet.

The adult will complete the following steps:

1. Write the child's name below their potato with a permanent marker.
2. Once the baking sheet is full, the potatoes are baked for approximately 20 minutes.

GROUP SIZE:

3–5 children

24

Easter Bread

AGES: 4–5

DEVELOPMENTAL GOALS:

- ✂ To recognize colors
- ✂ To create equal pieces

LEARNING OBJECTIVE:

The child will practice color recognition and divide dough equally to make Easter bread.

MATERIALS:

Ingredients	Equipment
Eggs (save carton)	Large pan for boiling eggs
Water	Paper towels
Food coloring	Cups
Frozen bread dough	Tablespoon (measuring)
Vinegar	Tablespoon (stirring)
	Baking sheet
	Aluminum foil
	Permanent marker
	Cloth to cover baking sheet

ADULT PREPARATION (DAY 1):

1. Cover eggs with water in a large pan. Boil eggs for three minutes. Cook one egg per child plus several extras to use as replacements for any eggs that crack.

2. Put 1 cup water, 1 tablespoon of vinegar, and food coloring into different cups.

continued

Easter Bread continued

3. Set a boiled egg in each color. Leave the egg in the coloring until the color of the egg reaches the desired hue.

4. Place the eggs on a paper towel to absorb the color that drains off the eggs.

5. Place the eggs back in the egg carton. Put the eggs in the refrigerator.

6. Thaw the bread dough in the refrigerator overnight.

ADULT PREPARATION (DAY 2):

1. Cover the baking sheet with aluminum foil.

2. Tear or cut a sheet of aluminum foil approximately 12–15" in length for each child.

3. Divide the bread dough into equal portions for each child.

PROCEDURES:

The child will complete the following steps:

1. Wash hands.

2. Set a sheet of aluminum foil on the table.

3. Place his or her dough on the aluminum foil.

4. Break his or her dough into three equal pieces.

5. Roll his or her three pieces of dough into ropes, attempting to make three ropes of equal length.

6. Attempt to braid or weave the three pieces of "rope" together.

7. Select a colored boiled egg and identify the color.

8. Wrap the woven dough around the egg, making a nest for the egg.

9. Place the dough-wrapped egg on the foil-covered baking sheet, with adult assistance.

The adult will complete the following steps:

1. Space the children's Easter breads about three inches apart on the baking sheet.

2. Write each child's name below his or her bread with a permanent marker.

3. When the baking sheet is full, cover the bread with a clean cloth. Set the baking sheet aside to let the dough rise for approximately one hour.

4. After the dough has risen, put the bread into the oven for about 30 minutes or until golden brown.

continued

Easter Bread continued

Note: Children may help color the eggs (Day 1 of adult preparation).

To use less bread dough or if children have difficulty braiding the dough, simply have each child make two ropes of dough and then twist it. If the dough is sticky, rub a little bit of flour on hands.

⚠ SAFETY PRECAUTION:

Always wash your hands and have the children wash their hands after handling eggs. If Easter bread is not refrigerated, do not eat the eggs.

GROUP SIZE:

4–5 children

Egg and Ham Burrito

AGES: 3–5

DEVELOPMENTAL GOALS:

- ✂ To stimulate small motor skills
- ✂ To observe a transformation

LEARNING OBJECTIVE:

The child will stimulate small muscles while cutting and observing the transformation between the raw and cooked eggs.

MATERIALS:

Ingredients	Equipment
Eggs (one per child)	Electric skillet (nonstick)
Cooking spray	Tape to secure the electric
Sliced ham (half slice per child)	skillet's cord to table and floor
Small flour tortillas (one per child)	Wooden spoon
Shredded cheese (optional)	Forks
	Cups
	Plates
	Plastic knives
	Towels

ADULT PREPARATION:

1. Cut the ham slices in half and place one on each child's plate.
2. Set materials on table.
3. Place a half ham slice and plastic knife on a plate for each child.

continued

Egg and Ham Burrito continued

4. Secure the cord of the electric skillet with tape on the table and floor.
5. Roll towels and place them around the electric skillet.
6. Lightly spray the skillet with cooking spray to prevent the egg from sticking.
7. Turn the skillet to medium heat.

PROCEDURES:

The child will complete the following steps:

1. Wash hands.
2. Select a plate with half a ham slice and a plastic knife.
3. Cut the ham into pieces.
4. Set the ham aside.
5. Select an egg.
6. Crack the egg, with adult assistance, and put it in a cup.
7. Place the cut ham into the egg mixture and stir with a fork.
8. Pour the mixture into the skillet, with adult assistance.
9. Using a wooden spoon, stir the egg and ham mixture until the egg is thoroughly cooked.
10. Place a flour tortilla on the plate.
11. Watch as the adult removes the egg mixture from the skillet and places it on the tortilla.
12. Optional: Sprinkle the egg mixture with shredded cheese and then roll the mixture into a burrito.

Note: All the children's egg mixtures may be blended together and cooked at one time in a kitchen. Doing this will allow all children to sit and eat their egg burritos together.

SUBSTITUTION:

One-fourth cup of egg substitute per child may be used instead of handling and cracking eggs.

SAFETY PRECAUTION:

Maintain close supervision when using a heat source. Do not leave it unattended. Always wash your hands and have the children wash their hands after handling eggs.

GROUP SIZE:

2–3 children

Enchiladas

DEVELOPMENTAL GOALS:

✁ To stimulate the muscles in the hand

✁ To experience new foods

LEARNING OBJECTIVE:

The child will stimulate hand muscles while creating an enchilada.

MATERIALS:

Ingredients	Equipment
Ground beef	Spoons
Taco seasoning mix	Plate
Enchilada sauce	Bowls
Water	Skillet
Shredded cheese	Colander
Corn tortillas	Child-size pitcher
	Baking sheet
	Aluminum foil
	Permanent marker

ADULT PREPARATION:

1. Cook ground beef in a skillet until brown.
2. Using a colander, drain excess grease into a small bowl.
3. Return beef to the skillet and add the taco mixture, following the package directions.
4. Place beef and shredded cheese in separate bowls.
5. Place corn tortillas on a plate.
6. Place the enchilada sauce in a child-size pitcher.

continued

Enchiladas continued

7. Cover baking sheet with aluminum foil.
8. Preheat the oven to 350°.

PROCEDURES:

The child will complete the following steps:

1. Wash hands.
2. Place a corn tortilla on a plate.
3. Spoon beef mixture down the center of the corn tortilla.
4. Sprinkle shredded cheese on top of the beef.
5. Fold the ends of the tortilla over each other.
6. Put the enchilada seam down on the foil-covered baking sheet, with adult assistance if needed.
7. Carefully pour sauce to cover the enchilada.
8. Sprinkle shredded cheese on top of the enchilada.

The adult will complete the following:

1. Write the child's name on the edge of the foil-covered baking sheet.
2. Bake the enchilada for 5–10 minutes, until the cheese is melted.

VEGETARIAN SUBSTITUTION:

Omit the beef and simply use additional cheese, or replace the beef with meatless ground burger (found in the frozen foods aisle of the grocery store).

GROUP SIZE:

3–5 children

F

Flower Biscuits

DEVELOPMENTAL GOALS:

✂ To use a knife safely

✂ To follow directions

LEARNING OBJECTIVE:

The child will practice cutting skills and follow directions while making flower biscuits.

MATERIALS:

Ingredients	Equipment
Canned biscuits (one biscuit per child) Jelly	Baking sheet Aluminum foil Permanent marker Plastic knife Spoon Plates Bowl

ADULT PREPARATION:

1. Cover a baking sheet with aluminum foil.
2. Place jelly in a bowl.
3. Put a biscuit and plastic knife on a plate for each child.
4. Preheat the oven to 425°.

continued

32

Flower Biscuits continued

PROCEDURES:

The child will complete the following steps:

1. Wash hands.

2. Select a plate with a biscuit and plastic knife.

3. Use a thumb to make an indentation in the center of the biscuit.

4. Use the knife to cut slits in the biscuit. The slits will run from the outside of the biscuit to the start of the thumb indentation and should be cut all the way through the biscuit to the plate. (These slits will bake apart, forming flower petals.) Avoid cutting the thumb indentation, because this is where the jelly will rest.

5. Place a spoonful of jelly in the thumb indentation.

6. Move the biscuit to the foil-covered baking sheet, with adult assistance.

The adult will complete the following steps:

1. Write the child's name below his or her biscuit, with a permanent marker.

2. Leave one to two inches between biscuits, to prevent them from joining when they bake.

3. When the baking sheet is full, put the biscuits in the oven, baking them for 10–12 minutes or until golden brown.

Note: A piece of fruit may be substituted for the jelly.

GROUP SIZE:

2–5 children

Fruit and Cheese Sailboat

DEVELOPMENTAL GOALS:

✄ To follow a sequence

✄ To provide a nutritious snack

LEARNING OBJECTIVE:

The child will follow a sequence of steps to make a nutritious snack.

MATERIALS:

Ingredients	Equipment
Small bananas Individually wrapped cheese slices Pretzel rods	Plates Knife Picture of a sailboat

ADULT PREPARATION:

1. Slice the cheese in half, creating two triangles. Cut enough for each child to have one triangle of cheese.
2. Cut the top off the banana to enable the child to peel the skin away.

continued

Fruit and Cheese Sailboat continued

3. Break pretzel rods in half. Each child will have a half rod.
4. Place a half pretzel rod, a triangle of cheese, and a banana on each plate.
5. Set a picture of a sailboat on the table.

PROCEDURES:

The child will complete the following steps:

1. Wash hands.
2. Look at the picture of the sailboat.
3. Peel his or her banana. The adult will assist if necessary.
4. Lay his or her banana horizontally toward the bottom of the plate.
5. Lay the pretzel half on the plate, positioning it perpendicular to the banana.
6. Take the plastic wrap off the cheese triangle and lay the cheese over the pretzel rod.

Note: For younger children, use only half of a banana per child.

GROUP SIZE:

2–5 children

Fruit Smoothie

DEVELOPMENTAL GOALS:

- ✂ To participate in a small group activity
- ✂ To share cooking duties

LEARNING OBJECTIVE:

The child will share cooking duties while making fruit smoothies in a small group.

MATERIALS:

Ingredients	Equipment
Cold milk	Blender
Peach yogurt (8-ounce carton)	Measuring cup
Chilled sliced peaches	Measuring spoon
(15-ounce can)	Smooth-edge can opener
Vanilla	Colander
	Spoon
	Cups
	Child-size pitcher
	Tape to secure electrical cord

ADULT PREPARATION:

1. Open the can of chilled sliced peaches.
2. Drain the syrup from the peaches using a colander, then put the peaches in a cup.

continued

Fruit Smoothie continued

3. Pour 1 cup cold milk into a child-size pitcher.

4. Open carton of peach yogurt

5. Place blender on the table.

6. Secure the electrical cord to the table and floor with tape.

PROCEDURES:

The children will complete the following steps:

1. Wash hands.

2. Take turns adding the following ingredients to the blender:

   a. The chilled peaches (from the cup)

   b. The cup of milk (from the pitcher)

   c. The peach yogurt (from the carton)

   d. ¼ teaspoon of vanilla

The adult will complete the following steps

1. Turn the blender on medium speed for approximately 1 minute or until the contents are smoothly blended.

2. Pour the mixture into cups.

Note: This makes six ½ cup servings.

GROUP SIZE:

4–5 children

Goldfish Pond

AGES: 2–5

DEVELOPMENTAL GOALS:

✂ To create a fun snack

✂ To practice counting

LEARNING OBJECTIVE:

The child will measure and count while making a fun snack that resembles a goldfish bowl.

MATERIALS:

Ingredients	Equipment
Large package blue gelatin mix (14 tablespoons) Water Gummy fish	Glass measuring cup Spoon Cups Measuring spoons Masking tape Permanent marker Tray

ADULT PREPARATION:

1. Heat 3½ cups water in the microwave for 4–5 minutes. Do not boil.
2. Put blue gelatin mix into a bowl.
3. Put gummy fish in a bowl.
4. Write the child's name on a section of masking tape.
5. Place the name tape on individual cups.
6. Pour ½ cup hot water into plastic measuring cup.

continued

Goldfish Pond continued

PROCEDURES:

The child will complete the following steps:

1. Wash hands.
2. Measure and mix 2 tablespoons gelatin mix and ½ cup of hot water (with adult assistance) in a small cup. Stir until the gelatin is dissolved.
3. Count out a predetermined number of fish.
4. Add the fish to the cup of gelatin.

The adult will complete the following steps:

1. Put each child's cup on a tray.
2. Refrigerate the tray of gelatin and fish overnight.

SAFETY PRECAUTION:

Supervise children closely when using gummy fish to prevent choking. Assist children when pouring hot water.

GROUP SIZE:

2–5 children

Grass Cake

AGES: 2–5

DEVELOPMENTAL GOALS:

✂ To promote fine motor skills

✂ To enhance social development

LEARNING OBJECTIVE:

The children will poke, pour, and take turns while making a grass cake.

MATERIALS:

Ingredients	Equipment
Box of chocolate cake mix	Resealable plastic bag
Vegetable oil	Cake pan
Water	Mixing bowl
Eggs	Electric mixer
Bag of shredded coconut flakes	Measuring cups
Green food coloring	9" x 13" cake pan
14-ounce can sweetened	Resealable plastic bag
condensed milk	Chopsticks
Whipped topping	Child-size pitcher
	Spoons
	Smocks

continued

Grass Cake continued

ADULT PREPARATION:

1. Follow the directions on the cake mix, using vegetable oil, eggs, water, and measuring cups to bake a chocolate cake.
2. Let the cake cool.
3. Pour a can of evaporated milk into a child-size pitcher.
4. Put a small package of shredded coconut into a resealable plastic bag.
5. Squirt green food coloring into the bag and squish the color throughout the coconut.
6. Lay the coconut on a paper towel to dry.
7. Put the coconut into a bowl.

PROCEDURES:

The children will complete the following steps:

1. Wash hands.
2. Wear smocks.
3. Add the green food coloring to the whipped topping and stir, mixing the color throughout the topping.
4. Use chopsticks to poke holes all over the cake.
5. Take turns slowly pouring milk all over the cake.
6. When the cake has absorbed the milk, take turns frosting the cake with green tinted whipped topping.
7. Take turns sprinkling the green coconut over the cake.

Notes: Children may help mix the cake batter. If any children have an allergy to coconut, delete this ingredient.

GROUP SIZE:

6–12 children

Ground Beef Pie

DEVELOPMENTAL GOALS:

- ✄ To follow directions
- ✄ To layer ingredients

LEARNING OBJECTIVE:

The child will follow directions in layering the ingredients to make ground beef pie.

MATERIALS:

Ingredients	Equipment
Pastry tart shells (found in frozen foods aisle of grocery store)	2-quart microwave bowl
1 pound ground beef	Stirring spoon
Instant potatoes	Measuring spoon (tablespoon)
Milk	¼-cup measure
Water	Baking sheet
Butter	Permanent marker
15-ounce can green peas (optional)	Bowls
Shredded cheddar cheese	Colander

continued

Ground Beef Pie continued

ADULT PREPARATION:

1. Preheat oven to 350°.
2. Brown ground beef.
3. Use a colander to drain the grease from the ground beef.
4. Put the ground beef in a bowl.
5. Follow the microwave directions on the can or box of instant potatoes. Make the amount for four servings, which will feed eight children.
6. Optional: Drain the liquid from the can of peas, and place the peas in a bowl.
7. Put the shredded cheddar cheese in a separate bowl.
8. Write the child's name, with a permanent marker, on the bottom of the aluminum-foil pan containing the tart shell.
9. Follow the directions on the tart package; shells may need to be prebaked.

PROCEDURES:

The child will complete the following steps:

1. Wash hands.
2. Find the tart shell with his or her name written on the bottom.
3. Measure 1 tablespoon of ground beef into the tart shell.
4. Optional: measure 1 tablespoon of peas onto the ground beef.
5. Measure 2 tablespoons of mashed potatoes and place it on top of the beef.
6. Smooth the potatoes over the ground beef, using a spoon.
7. Top the mixture with 2 teaspoons of shredded cheddar cheese.
8. Place the tart on top of the baking sheet.

The adult will complete the following step:

1. When the baking sheet is full, bake the tarts for approximately 20 minutes.

VEGETARIAN SUBSTITUTION:

Use meatless ground burger (found in the frozen foods aisle of the grocery store) in place of ground beef.

GROUP SIZE:

3–5 children

Ham and Cheese Bread

DEVELOPMENTAL GOALS:

✄ To stimulate small muscle development

✄ To promote self-help skills

LEARNING OBJECTIVE:

The child will use small muscles while making an individual serving of ham and cheese bread.

MATERIALS:

Ingredients	Equipment
Frozen bread dough	Baking sheet
Package of sliced ham	Small cotton towel to cover the dough
Block of cheddar or mozzarella cheese	Aluminum foil
Melted butter	Permanent marker
	Child-size rolling pins
	Knife
	Bowls
	Small bowl for butter
	Pastry brush

continued

Ham and Cheese Bread continued

ADULT PREPARATION:

1. Thaw bread dough in the refrigerator overnight.
2. Cover baking sheet with aluminum foil.
3. Cut ham into bite-size pieces and place them in a bowl.
4. Cut cheese into bite-size pieces and place them in a bowl.
5. Tear off 12"–15" pieces of aluminum foil for each child.
6. Write each child's name on a piece of foil.
7. Preheat the oven to 350°.

PROCEDURES:

The child will complete the following steps:

1. Wash hands.
2. Select the piece of aluminum foil with his or her name.
3. Place a section of bread dough on the foil and roll the dough flat, using a rolling pin.
4. Sprinkle ham and cheese over the bread dough.
5. Roll the dough into a loaf.
6. Place the dough seam side down on the foil covered baking sheet, with adult assistance.

The adult will complete the following steps:

1. Write the child's name below the dough, leaving approximately three to four inches between loaves.
2. Once the baking sheet is full, cover the dough with a clean cloth. Set aside to rise for approximately one hour.
3. Once the dough has risen, place the baking sheet in the oven for approximately 35–40 minutes or until the bread is golden brown.
4. Brush the dough with melted butter upon removing it from the oven.

GROUP SIZE:

2–5 children

Ham Roll-Ups

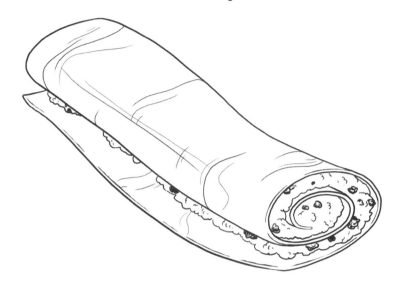

AGES: 3–5

DEVELOPMENTAL GOALS:

✂ To introduce the use of a knife for spreading

✂ To provide a healthy snack

LEARNING OBJECTIVE:

The child will practice spreading with a knife while making a healthy snack.

MATERIALS:

Ingredients	Equipment
Package of sliced sandwich ham Whipped cream cheese Fresh broccoli florets	Paper plates Permanent marker Plastic knives Colander Chopper Cutting board

ADULT PREPARATION:

1. Place broccoli florets in a colander.
2. Run water over the broccoli to clean it, then set it aside to dry.
3. Place a slice of ham and a plastic knife on a plate for each child.

PROCEDURES:

The child will complete the following steps:

1. Wash hands.
2. Select a plate with ham and a plastic knife.

continued

Ham Roll-Ups continued

3. Spread whipped cream cheese on the slice of ham with the plastic knife.
4. Place a broccoli floret on the cutting board and place the chopper over the broccoli.
5. Chop up a floret of broccoli using the chopper.
6. Sprinkle the chopped broccoli on top of the ham and cream cheese.
7. Roll up the ham, with the cream cheese and broccoli inside.

The adult will complete the following steps:

1. Write the child's name on the edge of his or her plate with the permanent marker.
2. Place the ham roll-ups in the refrigerator until snack time.

VEGETARIAN SUBSTITUTION:

Use a leaf of lettuce in place of the ham.

GROUP SIZE:

2–5 children

Heart Cinnamon Toast

DEVELOPMENTAL GOALS:

- ✂ To stimulate fine motor skills
- ✂ To develop eye-hand coordination

LEARNING OBJECTIVE:

The child will use a knife and cookie cutter to stimulate fine motor skills while making heart-shaped cinnamon toast.

MATERIALS:

Ingredients	Equipment
Sliced bread Softened butter or margarine in a small tub Cinnamon Sugar	Baking sheet Aluminum foil Permanent marker Plates Heart-shaped cookie cutter Plastic knives Bowls Spoon Funnel Plastic container with holes in the lid such as an empty salt shaker.

ADULT PREPARATION:

1. Cover a baking sheet with aluminum foil.
2. Put sugar and cinnamon in a bowl and use a spoon to mix well.

continued

Heart Cinnamon Toast continued

3. Using the funnel, pour the cinnamon sugar into the shaker.

4. Secure the lid on the shaker.

5. Place a slice of bread and a plastic knife on a plate for each child.

6. Set ingredients and equipment on the table.

7. Preheat the oven to broil.

PROCEDURES:

The child will complete the following steps:

1. Wash hands.

2. Select a plate with a plastic knife and a slice of bread.

3. Use the cookie cutter to cut a heart-shaped piece of bread.

4. Leave the bread heart on the plate; place the bread scraps in a bowl.

5. Using the plastic knife, spread butter or margarine on the bread.

6. Use the shaker and sprinkle cinnamon sugar on the bread.

The adult will complete the following steps:

1. Place the bread on the foil-covered baking sheet.

2. Write the child's name below the heart bread.

3. Once the baking sheet is full, broil the bread in the oven for approximately 3–5 minutes.

Note: Bread crust may be fed to the birds.

GROUP SIZE:

2–5 children

Ice Cream Sandwich

DEVELOPMENTAL GOALS:

- ✄ To develop the small muscles
- ✄ To recognize a square

LEARNING OBJECTIVE:

The child will identify a square while using small muscles to make an ice cream sandwich.

MATERIALS:

Ingredients	Equipment
Vanilla ice cream Graham crackers	Plastic knives Resealable plastic bags (sandwich size) Permanent marker Plates Bowls

ADULT PREPARATION:

1. Break each graham cracker in half to form two squares.
2. Place a heaping tablespoon of softened ice cream in a bowl for each child.
3. Set two graham cracker halves and a plastic knife on each plate.

continued

Ice Cream Sandwich continued

PROCEDURES:

The child will complete the following steps:

1. Wash hands.
2. Identify the shape of a graham cracker half as a square.
3. Select a bowl of ice cream, a plate with two graham cracker halves, and a knife.
4. Spread the ice cream on one of the graham cracker squares, using a knife.
5. Place the second graham cracker square on top of the ice cream.

The adult will complete the following steps:

1. Write the child's name on a resealable plastic bag.
2. Place the ice cream sandwich into the plastic bag.
3. Seal the bag and put it in the freezer.

GROUP SIZE:

1–5 children

Igloo

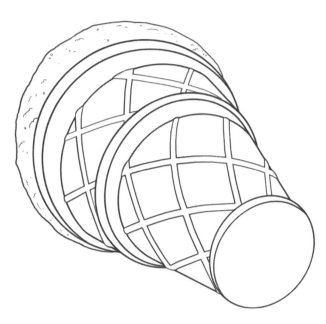

DEVELOPMENTAL GOALS:

✄ To participate in a group activity

✄ To develop measurement skills

LEARNING OBJECTIVE:

The children will participate in a group to measure ingredients and make an edible igloo.

MATERIALS:

Ingredients	Equipment
White cake mix	Large bowl
Eggs	Muffin tin
Oil	Aluminum foil
Water	Permanent marker
Ice cream cones (cake cones)	Egg beater
Whipped topping	Spoons
	Plates

ADULT PREPARATION:

1. Tear aluminum foil into 5" square sheets.
2. Write each child's name on a sheet of foil with a permanent marker.
3. Set out box of white cake mix.
4. Set out eggs, water, and oil as the cake mix directions require.
5. Preheat the oven to 350°.

continued

Igloo continued

PROCEDURES:

The children will complete the following steps:

1. Wash hands.
2. Take turns adding and mixing cake ingredients according to package directions.
3. Use an egg beater to mix the batter.
4. Take turns filling an ice cream cone with the cake batter.
5. Select the foil square with his or her name.

The adult will complete the following steps:

1. Scrunch the foil around the bottom of the cone (to prevent the cone from falling over) and then place it standing upright in the muffin tin.
2. When the muffin tin is full, place the cones with cake batter in the oven and bake for 20–25 minutes.
3. Insert a toothpick into the cake. It will come out clean when baking is finished.
4. Allow the cones to cool. Once they are cool, lay them on their sides on individual plates.
5. Remove the aluminum foil, and write each child's name on his or her plate.
6. Help the children frost their igloos, using spoons and whipped topping.

GROUP SIZE:

4–6 children

Initial Bread

AGES: 3–5

DEVELOPMENTAL GOALS:

- ✄ To recognize the first letter of his or her name
- ✄ To stimulate the muscles in the hands

LEARNING OBJECTIVE:

The child will recognize the first initial of his or her name while making bread shaped like that letter.

MATERIALS:

Ingredients	Equipment
Canned bread twists	Baking sheet Aluminum foil Wax paper Permanent marker Paper plates

ADULT PREPARATION:

1. Preheat the oven to 400°.
2. Cover a baking sheet with aluminum foil.
3. Write child's first initial on a paper plate with a marker.
4. Tear a 7" sheet of wax paper for each child.
5. Open the can of bread twists, separate the twists, and place them on a separate plate covered with wax paper.

continued

Initial Bread continued

PROCEDURES:

The child will complete the following steps:

1. Wash hands.
2. Listen to the adult explain that the first letter of someone's name is an initial.
3. Select the plate with the first letter of his or her name; identify the letter.
4. Cover the plate with wax paper.
5. Select a section of dough and roll the dough stretching the twist longer.
6. Follow the outline of the letter beneath the wax paper to trace the initial with dough.

The adult will complete the following steps:

1. Lift the letter-shaped dough off the wax paper and onto the baking sheet covered with foil.
2. Use a permanent marker to write the child's name below the dough.
3. Space initials approximately two inches apart on the baking sheet.
4. Once the baking sheet is full, bake the dough for approximately 10–12 minutes or until golden brown.

GROUP SIZE:

3–5 children

Jelly Rolls

AGES: 3–5

DEVELOPMENTAL GOALS:

✂ To promote eye-hand coordination

✂ To recognize a triangle

LEARNING OBJECTIVE:

The child will recognize a triangle shape and improve eye-hand coordination while making jelly rolls.

MATERIALS:

Ingredients	Equipment
Crescent roll dough (found in cans in the grocery store's dairy case) Jelly	Plates Baking sheet Aluminum foil Permanent marker Plastic knives Bowl

ADULT PREPARATION:

1. Preheat the oven to 400°.
2. Cover the baking sheet with aluminum foil.
3. Place the jelly in a bowl.
4. Place a triangle of crescent roll dough and a plastic knife on each child's plate.

continued

Jelly Rolls continued

PROCEDURES:

The child will complete the following steps:

1. Wash hands.
2. Select a plate with a knife and a flat triangle of crescent roll dough.
3. Identify the shape of the dough.
4. Use the knife to spread the jelly on the crescent roll dough.
5. After spreading jelly, roll the dough into a log shape by starting with the pointed end of the triangle.

The adult will complete the following steps:

1. Place the rolled dough onto the foil covered baking sheet.
2. Write the child's name below the dough.
3. Space the dough two inches apart.
4. Bake for approximately 12–15 minutes, until the dough is golden brown.

GROUP SIZE:

1–6 children

Juice Bars

AGES: 2–5

DEVELOPMENTAL GOALS:

✂ To recognize name

✂ To provide a nutritious snack

LEARNING OBJECTIVE:

The child will participate in making a nutritious snack and will recognize his or her name while preparing a juice bar.

MATERIALS:

Ingredients	Equipment
100% fruit juice	Small paper cups Muffin tin or cake pan Child-size pitcher Craft sticks Permanent marker

ADULT PREPARATION (DAY 1):

1. Pour juice into child-size pitchers.

2. Using a permanent marker, label the bottom of the cups with the children's names.

3. Label the top of a craft stick with each child's name.

4. Set the craft sticks on a plate.

continued

Juice Bars continued

PROCEDURES (DAY 1):

The child will complete the following steps:

1. Wash hands.
2. Find the cup with his or her name written on the bottom.
3. Pour juice into the cup, filling it three-fourths full.
4. Find the craft stick with his or her name on it and place it in his or her cup. (The writing on the craft stick should be above the juice.)

The adult will complete the following steps:

1. Place the juice cups in a muffin tin or cake pan, to prevent the juice from tipping over in the freezer.
2. Freeze the juice cups overnight.

ADULT PREPARATION (DAY 2):

1. Place the juice bars on the table at snack time.

PROCEDURES (DAY 2):

The child will complete the following steps:

1. Find his or her juice bar by identifying the name on the craft stick.
2. Remove the paper cup from the frozen juice before eating it.

GROUP SIZE:

2–5 children

Just Smile

AGES: 4–5

DEVELOPMENTAL GOALS:

- ✄ To develop self-help skills
- ✄ To enhance eye-hand coordination

LEARNING OBJECTIVE:

The child will use a knife to spread and make an apple treat that resembles a smile.

MATERIALS:

Ingredients	Equipment
Red apples	Bowl
Lemon juice	Tablespoon (measuring)
Water	Paper plates
Creamy peanut butter	Paring knife
Golden raisins	Plastic knives
	Two bowls
	Permanent marker
	Mirror

ADULT PREPARATION:

1. Wash the apples.
2. Use the paring knife to core the apples and cut them into quarters, and place them in a bowl.
3. Pour 2 tablespoons of lemon juice over the apples. Add water until the fruit is covered. Stir with a spoon. (This will prevent the fruit from turning brown.)
4. Put creamy peanut butter in a bowl.
5. Put raisins in a separate bowl.

continued

Just Smile continued

6. Write the children's names on individual paper plates with a permanent marker.

7. Drain the apples and place them on a plate.

PROCEDURES:

The child will complete the following steps:

1. Look in a mirror and count how many teeth he or she has.
2. Wash hands.
3. Select a quarter of an apple and place it on the plate.
4. Use the plastic knife to spread peanut butter on the apple.
5. Count the number of raisins equal to the number of teeth.
6. Place the raisins on the apple slice to resemble teeth.

Note: If a child is allergic to peanut butter, use a caramel spread as a substitute.

⚠ SAFETY PRECAUTION:

Supervise children closely when using raisins, which are a choking hazard.

GROUP SIZE:

2–5 children

Kabobs

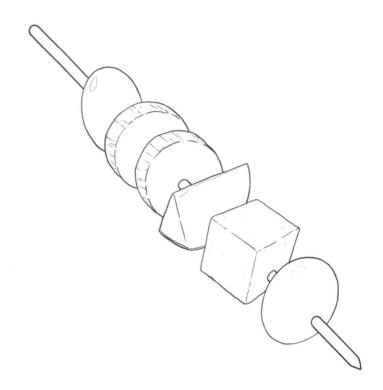

AGES: 3–5

DEVELOPMENTAL GOALS:

- ✄ To develop small muscles
- ✄ To promote eye-hand coordination

LEARNING OBJECTIVE:

The child will develop small muscles and eye-hand coordination while placing fruit on a skewer to make a kabob.

MATERIALS:

Ingredients	Equipment
Lemon juice	Bowls
Water	Tablespoon (measuring)
Apples	Wooden skewers
Bananas	Paper plates
Seedless grapes	Permanent marker
Cheese	Spoons or forks
	Knife
	Cutting board
	Colander

ADULT PREPARATION:

1. Cut apples, bananas, and cheese into bite-size pieces.
2. Place the grapes, apples, bananas, and cheese in separate bowls.

continued

Kabobs continued

3. Pour 2 tablespoons of lemon juice over the apples and bananas. Add water until the fruit is covered. Stir with a spoon. (This will prevent the fruit from turning brown.)

4. Write children's names on the edges of individual paper plates.

5. Using a colander, drain the water and lemon juice from the apples and bananas. Return the fruits to their individual bowls.

6. Place all materials on the table.

PROCEDURES:

The child will complete the following steps:

1. Wash hands.

2. Select the plate with his or her name on it.

3. Spoon two or three pieces of each fruit and cheese onto the plate.

4. Place each piece of fruit and cheese onto the wooden skewer.

EXPANSION:

Four- and five-year-olds may place the fruit and cheese onto the skewers in a pattern.

GROUP SIZE:

3–4 children

Kiwi Strawnana Slush

DEVELOPMENTAL GOALS:

* To practice eye-hand coordination
* To develop self-help skills

LEARNING OBJECTIVE:

The child will use a knife to cut ingredients and will then measure and add them to a blender to make a slush.

MATERIALS:

Ingredients	Equipment
Kiwi (½ per child) Strawberries (2–3 per child) Banana (2" piece per child) Apple juice	Plates Paring knife (adult) Plastic knives (children) Tablespoon (measuring) Bowls Blender Cups

ADULT PREPARATION:

1. Wash kiwi and strawberries.
2. Peel kiwi with a paring knife and cut in half.
3. Remove green stem from strawberries.
4. Place kiwi and strawberries in separate bowls.
5. Cut banana into 2" sections. Leave peel on.
6. Put bananas in a third bowl.
7. Pour apple juice in a separate bowl.

continued

Kiwi Strawnana Slush continued

PROCEDURES:

The child will complete the following steps:

1. Wash hands.
2. Select a kiwi half and place it on plate.
3. Slice kiwi into smaller pieces with a plastic knife.
4. Add kiwi to the blender.
5. Count out 2–3 strawberries (2 large or 3 regular) and place them on the plate.
6. Cut the strawberries in half with the plastic knife.
7. Add the strawberries to the blender.
8. Peel a section of banana and put it on the plate to cut into slices.
9. Add the banana slices to the blender.
10. Dip measuring spoon into the bowl of apple juice and measure out 2 tablespoons of juice, then add the juice to the blender.

The adult will complete the following steps:

1. Place the lid on the blender.
2. Select a chop or purify setting to mix the ingredients.
3. When the mixture is completely blended, pour the kiwi strawnana slush into a cup.

Note: Fruit and juice may be chilled prior to use, to make a cold slush.

GROUP SIZE:

2–4 children

Kolache

AGES: 3–5

DEVELOPMENTAL GOALS:

✂ To recognize food from other cultures

✂ To follow directions

LEARNING OBJECTIVE:

The child will follow directions to make a kolache, a food from another culture.

MATERIALS:

Ingredients	Equipment
Frozen bread dough Jam (peach, strawberry, or apricot)	Wax paper Globe or world map Kitchen scissors Bowl Spoons Baking sheet Aluminum foil Permanent marker

ADULT PREPARATION:

1. Preheat the oven to 350°.
2. Cover the baking sheet with aluminum foil.
3. Place jam in a bowl.
4. Use a pair of kitchen scissors to cut the dough into at least 12 portions.

PROCEDURES:

The child will complete the following steps:

1. Wash hands.
2. With adult help, find the area he or she lives in on a globe.

continued

Kolache continued

3. With adult help, point to Czechoslovakia and listen as the adult tells him or her that they will be making kolaches (coe-lah-chees), which are from that country.

4. Select a sheet of wax paper.

5. Place a section of dough on the wax paper.

6. Knead the dough, following the adult's example.

7. Roll his or her dough into a ball.

8. Use the palm of the hand and fingers to press the ball into a flat circle.

9. Use his or her fingers to make an indentation in the center of the dough circle.

10. Use a spoon to fill the indentation with jam.

The adult will complete the following steps:

1. Place the kolaches onto the foil-covered baking sheet.

2. Write the child's name below the kolache.

3. Space the kolaches approximately two inches apart on the baking sheet.

4. When the baking sheet is full, bake the kolaches for approximately 15–20 minutes, or until golden brown.

GROUP SIZE:

1–6 children

Lasagna

DEVELOPMENTAL GOALS:

- ✄ To use patterning in the placement of ingredients
- ✄ To stimulate eye-hand coordination

LEARNING OBJECTIVE:

The child will use patterning skills while layering ingredients to make lasagna.

MATERIALS:

Ingredients	Equipment
1 cup ricotta cheese 1¾ cup shredded mozzarella cheese ½ cup grated parmesan cheese 6 lasagna noodles 26-ounce jar of spaghetti sauce Water	Pot to boil lasagna noodles Plate Knife or kitchen scissors Bowls Muffin tin Foil muffin liners Large stirring spoon Measuring spoons Measuring cups Colander Permanent marker

ADULT PREPARATION:

1. Break lasagna noodles in half.
2. Boil lasagna noodles on the stove according to the package directions.

continued

Lasagna continued

3. Drain the pasta with a colander.

4. Run cool water over the pasta to help prevent the noodles from sticking together. Set noodles on a plate.

5. Preheat the oven to 350°.

6. Mix 1 cup ricotta cheese, 1 cup shredded mozzarella cheese, and ½ cup grated parmesan cheese in a bowl.

7. Put an additional ¾ cup of shredded mozzarella in another bowl.

8. Using the knife or kitchen scissors, cut the lasagna noodles into small pieces that will fit in a muffin liner.

9. Pour spaghetti sauce into a bowl.

10. Write the children's names on the bottoms of the foil muffin liners.

PROCEDURES:

The child will complete the following steps:

1. Wash hands.

2. Select the foil muffin liner with his or her name.

3. Measure and place 1 teaspoon of spaghetti sauce into the bottom of the foil liner.

4. Place one layer of lasagna noodle pieces in the muffin liner.

5. Measure 1 tablespoon of the cheese mixture and spread it flat with a spoon over the noodles.

6. Repeat the layers, as follows:

   a. 1 tablespoon sauce

   b. Pasta

   c. 1 tablespoon cheese

7. When the foil muffin liner is nearly full, end with 1 tablespoon of sauce and 1 tablespoon of shredded mozzarella cheese.

The adult will complete the following steps:

1. Place the foil liner in the muffin tin.

2. When the muffin tin is full, bake the lasagna for approximately 25 minutes or until the mixture is bubbly.

continued

Lasagna continued

Notes: Each child may be given half a lasagna noodle to tear instead of the adult cutting it. The paper liners that are inserted between the foil liners in the package should not be used. The lasagna will stick to the paper liners. This recipe makes enough to fill 12 muffin cups.

GROUP SIZE:

2–3 children

Layered Dip

AGES: 3–5

DEVELOPMENTAL GOALS:

✂ To follow directions

✂ To develop self-help skills

LEARNING OBJECTIVE:

The child will follow directions to make a snack.

MATERIALS:

Ingredients	Equipment
Sour cream	Foil muffin liners
Refried beans	Permanent markers
Mild salsa	Measuring spoons
Shredded cheddar cheese	Bowls
Baked nacho chips	Can opener

ADULT PREPARATION:

1. Open the packages or cans of all ingredients, with the exception of the chips.
2. Place the sour cream, refried beans, salsa, and cheese into separate bowls.
3. Label the bottoms of the foil liners with each child's name.

continued

Layered Dip continued

PROCEDURES:

The child will complete the following steps:

1. Wash hands.
2. Find the foil muffin liner with his or her name.
3. Measure 1 tablespoon of refried beans and spread it into the bottom of the foil muffin liner.
4. Measure and pour 1 tablespoon of salsa into the foil liner.
5. Measure 1 tablespoon of sour cream and spread it on top of the salsa.
6. Measure 1 tablespoon of shredded cheese and place it on top of the sour cream.

The adult will complete the following step:

1. Set the child's muffin liner on a tray in the refrigerator to be served with baked nacho chips at snack time.

GROUP SIZE:

3–5 children

Lazy Tossed Salad

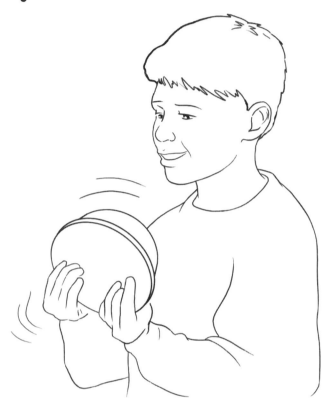

AGES: 3–5

DEVELOPMENTAL GOALS:

- ✂ To create a healthy snack
- ✂ To stimulate small muscle development

LEARNING OBJECTIVE:

The child will create a salad by mixing nutritious ingredients.

MATERIALS:

Ingredients	Equipment
Lettuce Cherry tomatoes Cucumbers Salad dressing	Plastic container with a lid (e.g., 15-ounce margarine container) Vegetable peeler Paring knife Cutting board Bowls Tablespoons

ADULT PREPARATION:

1. Cut the lettuce into small bite-size pieces.

2. Cut the cherry tomatoes into quarters.

3. Peel and cut the cucumbers into bite-size pieces.

continued

Lazy Tossed Salad continued

4. Place all ingredients in separate bowls.

5. Pour salad dressing in a separate bowl.

6. Place a tablespoon in each bowl.

PROCEDURES:

The child will complete the following steps:

1. Wash hands.

2. Add the following ingredients to the plastic container:

    a. 3 spoonfuls of lettuce

    b. 1 spoonful of tomatoes

    c. 1 spoonful of cucumbers

    d. ½ to 1 spoonful of dressing

3. Snap the lid on the container, using adult assistance if necessary.

4. Shake the container, thoroughly mixing the ingredients.

5. Pour the mixed salad into a bowl to eat.

SAFETY PRECAUTIONS:

Children must be closely supervised when using small cut foods, as they present a choking hazard.

GROUP SIZE:

3–5 children

Macaroni and Cheese

AGES: 3–5

DEVELOPMENTAL GOALS:

✀ To coordinate small and large muscles

✀ To provide a nutritious snack

LEARNING OBJECTIVE:

The child will pour and shake ingredients to help coordinate small and large muscles while making a nutritious snack of macaroni and cheese.

MATERIALS:

Ingredients	Equipment
Elbow macaroni Water Package of four types of shredded cheeses	Pot Spoon Bowl ¼-cup measure Measuring tablespoon Resealable sandwich-size bags Foil muffin liners Baking sheet or muffin tin Permanent marker Colander

ADULT PREPARATION:

1. Boil elbow macaroni according to package directions.
2. Drain the macaroni in a colander and place in a bowl.
3. Open the package of four cheeses and place in a separate bowl.
4. Using a permanent marker, label the bottoms of foil liners with children's names.

continued

Macaroni and Cheese continued

5. If the foil liners have paper inserts, remove them (the cheese will stick to the paper and tear it).

6. Preheat oven to 350°.

PROCEDURES:

The child will complete the following steps:

1. Wash hands.

2. Measure ¼ cup macaroni and place it in the resealable plastic bag.

3. Measure 2 tablespoons cheese and add it to the bag.

4. Seal the bag with adult help.

5. Shake the bag until the macaroni and cheese are well mixed.

The adult will complete the following steps:

1. Open the bag and pour it into the muffin liner with the child's name written on the bottom.

2. Set the foil liner on a tray or in a muffin tin.

3. Once the tray or tin is full, bake the macaroni for approximately 10 minutes, until all the cheese is melted.

GROUP SIZE:

3–5 children

Mexican Chicken

AGES: 3–5

DEVELOPMENTAL GOALS:

- ✂ To introduce new foods
- ✂ To develop fine motor coordination

LEARNING OBJECTIVE:

The child will develop his or her fine motor skills while being introduced to a new food as he or she makes Mexican chicken.

MATERIALS:

Ingredients	Equipment
Chicken Mild salsa Shredded Mexican cheese Water	¼-cup measure Tablespoon (measuring) Foil muffin liners Permanent marker Muffin tin Pan Knife Cutting board Bowls Plastic wrap

ADULT PREPARATION:

1. Boil chicken on the stove. This takes approximately one hour.
2. Allow the chicken to cool.
3. Remove the bones and skin from the chicken (unless you use boneless, skinless chicken).
4. Using a knife and cutting board, chop the chicken into small pieces.

continued

Mexican Chicken continued

5. Put the chicken in a bowl, cover with plastic wrap, and refrigerate until needed.

6. Preheat the oven to 350°.

7. Write the children's names on the bottoms of the foil liners with a permanent marker.

8. Pour the salsa and shredded cheese into separate bowls.

PROCEDURES:

The child will complete the following steps:

1. Wash hands.

2. Select the foil muffin liner with his or her name on the bottom.

3. Measure ¼ cup chicken and place it in the foil liner (may reduce to 3 tablespoons for three-year-olds.)

4. Measure 1 tablespoon of salsa and pour it over the chicken.

5. Measure 1 tablespoon of cheese and place it on top of the salsa.

The adult will complete the following steps:

1. Place the liner in the muffin tin.

2. Once the muffin tin is full, place the chicken in the oven for approximately 10–12 minutes. The cheese should be melted and the Mexican chicken should be sufficiently heated.

VEGETARIAN SUBSTITUTION:

Replace chicken with firm tofu cut into small pieces or meatless ground burger.

GROUP SIZE:

3–5 children

Monkey Bread

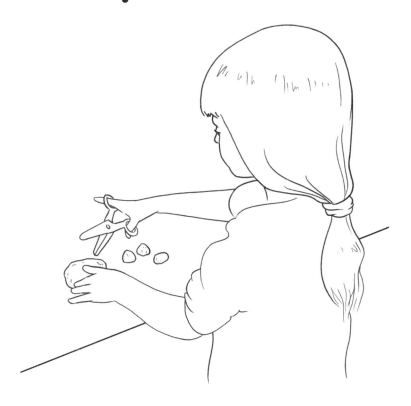

AGES: 2½–5

DEVELOPMENTAL GOALS:

- ✂ To encourage use of scissors
- ✂ To promote measurement

LEARNING OBJECTIVE:

The child will measure and cut the dough to make monkey bread.

MATERIALS:

Ingredients	Equipment
Canned biscuit dough Brown sugar Cinnamon Softened butter or margarine	Foil muffin liners Muffin tin Permanent marker Child-size scissors Measuring spoons Plates

ADULT PREPARATION:

1. Open the blades of child-size scissors and wash scissors in the dishwasher.
2. Write the children's names on the bottoms of individual foil muffin liners.
3. Place cinnamon, brown sugar, and softened butter or margarine in separate bowls.

continued

Monkey Bread continued

4. Place biscuit sections on individual plates.
5. Preheat oven to 400°.

PROCEDURES:

The child will complete the following steps:

1. Wash hands.
2. Select the muffin liner with his or her name written on the bottom.
3. Select a plate with a section of biscuit dough.
4. Using a pair of clean child-size scissors, cut the biscuit dough into smaller pieces.
5. Place the biscuit dough pieces in the foil liner.
6. Measure 1–2 teaspoons brown sugar and place it on top of the biscuit dough pieces.
7. Measure ⅛ teaspoon cinnamon and place it on top of the brown sugar.
8. Measure ½ teaspoon butter and place it on top of the cinnamon.

The adult will complete the following steps:

1. Place the muffin liner into the muffin tin.
2. Once the muffin tin is full, bake the monkey bread for approximately 12–15 minutes, until it is golden brown.

GROUP SIZE:

2–5 children

Nine-Ingredient Soup

AGES: 2–5

DEVELOPMENTAL GOALS:

✄ To promote social development

✄ To develop eye-hand coordination

LEARNING OBJECTIVE:

The children, working together in a small group, will take turns pouring ingredients into the pot to make a soup.

MATERIALS:

Ingredients	Equipment

15-ounce cans of:
  Potatoes
  Carrots
  Cut green beans
  Whole kernel corn
  Peas
  Vegetable broth
  Mild salsa
  Cheese spread (jar)
Milk
	Large pot
	Can opener
	Child-size pitcher
	Long-handled spoon
	Ladle
	Bowls
	Spoons

continued

Nine-Ingredient Soup continued

ADULT PREPARATION:

1. Open all cans and dispose of the lids.
2. Keep liquid in the cans.
3. Remove the lid from the jar of cheese.
4. Add 1 cup of milk to a child-size pitcher.

PROCEDURES:

The children will complete the following steps:

1. Wash hands.
2. Take turns adding the cans of ingredients (including liquids) to the pot.
3. Use a spoon to put the cheese in the pot.
4. Pour the milk into the pot.
5. Stir all the ingredients with a long-handled spoon.

The adult will complete the following step:

1. Take the pot to the kitchen and cook on low heat until the cheese is melted.

Note: If the children are present for a longer day, the soup may be cooked in a crockpot. Observe safety procedures and school policies.

SAFETY PRECAUTION:

If possible, use a smooth-edge can opener to prevent the children from accidentally getting cut by the edges of the cans. If a regular can opener is used, pour the ingredients into cups for the children to handle.

GROUP SIZE:

6–9 children

No-Bake Cookies

AGES: 3–5

DEVELOPMENTAL GOALS:

✂ To promote measuring skills

✂ To develop small muscles

LEARNING OBJECTIVE:

The child will measure and stir to make cookies without baking.

MATERIALS:

Ingredients	Equipment
Unsweetened cocoa powder Butter or margarine Milk Oatmeal (quick-cooking oats) Sugar	Electric skillet (nonstick) Tape to secure the electric skillet's cord to table and floor Measuring spoons Spoon Bowls Spatula Wax paper Tray or baking sheet Permanent marker Towels

ADULT PREPARATION:

1. Place milk, oats, cocoa, and softened butter or margarine in separate bowls.

2. Line a tray with wax paper.

continued

No-Bake Cookies continued

3. Secure the cord of the skillet with tape on the table and floor.

4. Roll towels and place around the outside of the electric skillet.

5. Plug the skillet in and preheat to medium, or 300°.

PROCEDURES:

The child will complete the following steps:

1. Measure and place the following ingredients in a bowl:

    a. 1 tablespoon plus 1 teaspoon sugar

    b. ¾ teaspoon cocoa powder

    c. 2 teaspoons softened butter or margarine

    d. 2 teaspoons milk

    e. ¼ cup quick-cooking oats

2. Stir the ingredients together.

3. Place the ingredients in the electric skillet, with adult help if needed.

4. Cook, stirring with a wooden spoon for approximately two to three minutes.

The adult will complete the following steps:

1. Remove the cookie from the skillet.

2. Place the cookie on the wax paper to set until firm.

3. Write the child's name below the cookie with a permanent marker.

Note: This recipe makes one large cookie or may be divided into two smaller cookies.

 ## SAFETY PRECAUTION:

When using heat, supervise the children closely to prevent burns.

GROUP SIZE:

1–2 children

Noodles

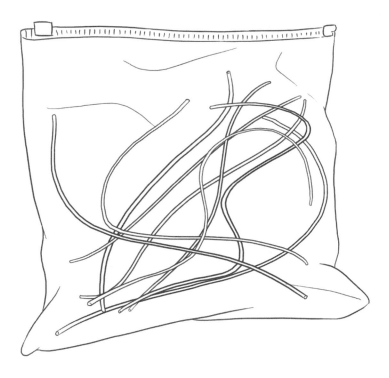

AGES: 4–5

DEVELOPMENTAL GOALS:

- ✂ To practice cooking procedures
- ✂ To stimulate eye-hand coordination

LEARNING OBJECTIVE:

The child will practice stirring, measuring, and rolling out ingredients while stimulating eye-hand coordination by making noodles.

MATERIALS:

Ingredients	Equipment
Flour Salt Egg substitute Milk	Child-size rolling pin Bowls ¼-cup measure Measuring spoons Fork Plastic knife Wax paper Permanent marker Resealable plastic bag

ADULT PREPARATION:

1. Place flour, milk, salt, and egg substitute in separate bowls.
2. Tear off one sheet of wax paper per child.

continued

Noodles continued

PROCEDURES:

The child will complete the following steps:

1. Wash hands.
2. Measure the following ingredients and place them in a bowl:
    a. 4 tablespoons flour
    b. ⅛ teaspoon salt
    c. ¾ teaspoon milk
    d. 1 tablespoon egg substitute
3. Mix all ingredients with a fork. Mix the ingredients well, forming dough.
4. Place the dough on wax paper.
5. Rub flour onto the rolling pin.
6. Roll the dough flat and very thin.
7. Carefully cut the dough into strips approximately ¼" wide. The adult may need to make marks in the dough to show the child how wide to cut. If the dough clings to the knife, allow it to sit for 10 minutes before cutting.

The adult will complete the following steps:

1. Write the child's name on the wax paper and set it aside.
2. Allow the dough to sit for approximately two hours before boiling. It may be placed in a plastic resealable bag and sent home for the family to cook. Refrigerate the noodles if they will not be cooked on the day they are made.
3. When ready to cook the noodles, boil water, then drop the noodles in the water for approximately 10 minutes.

GROUP SIZE:

1–2 children

Oatmeal Apple Crisp

AGES: 3–5

DEVELOPMENTAL GOALS:

- ✂ To practice cooking procedures
- ✂ To promote self-help skills

LEARNING OBJECTIVE:

The child will cut, measure, and mix to make oatmeal apple crisp.

MATERIALS:

Ingredients	Equipment
Quick-cooking oats	Measuring spoons
Flour	Forks
Butter or margarine	Foil muffin liners
Brown sugar	Permanent marker
Cinnamon	Tray or muffin tin
Apples (¼ apple per child, or ½ apple per child if apples are small)	Bowls
	Apple corer
	Plastic knives
Lemon juice	Plates
Water	

ADULT PREPARATION:

1. Wash apples; use an apple corer to slice and core apples; place the apples in a bowl.

continued

Oatmeal Apple Crisp continued

2. Pour 2 tablespoons of lemon juice over the apples. Add water until the fruit is covered. Stir with a spoon. (This will prevent the fruit from turning brown.)
3. Put flour, butter, brown sugar, cinnamon, and oats into separate bowls.
4. Using a permanent marker, label bottoms of foil liners with the children's names.
5. Preheat the oven to 350°.
6. Drain the apples.
7. Place ¼ apple and a plastic knife on a plate for each child.

PROCEDURES:

The child will complete the following steps:

1. Wash hands.
2. Select liner with his or her name written on the bottom.
3. Select a plate, plastic knife, and ¼ apple.
4. Cut the apple in smaller pieces on the plate.
5. Place the apple pieces in the foil liner.
6. Mix the following ingredients in a small bowl, using a fork:
   a. 2 teaspoons flour
   b. 2 teaspoons oats
   c. 2 teaspoons softened butter or margarine
   d. 1 tablespoon brown sugar
   e. ⅛ teaspoon cinnamon
7. Spread the mixture over the apples.

The adult will complete the following steps:

8. Put the foil liner on a tray or in a muffin tin.
9. When the tray or muffin tin is full, bake the oatmeal apple crisp for approximately 20 minutes.

GROUP SIZE:

3–5 children

Octopus Hot Dogs

AGES: 4–5

DEVELOPMENTAL GOALS:

✂ To observe a transformation

✂ To develop skill cutting with a knife

LEARNING OBJECTIVE:

The child will cut with a knife and observe a transformation while creating an octopus hot dog.

MATERIALS:

Ingredients	Equipment
Hot dogs (one per child) Water Catsup	Plates Plastic knives Pan Fork Tongs Colander

ADULT PREPARATION:

1. Put hot dogs on a plate.
2. Make an indentation, with a knife, approximately one inch from the end of each hot dog. This will be the child's measure to stop cutting.
3. Put the plates, plastic knives, and hot dogs on the table.
4. Place a pan filled halfway with water on the table.

continued

Octopus Hot Dogs continued

PROCEDURES:

The child will complete the following steps:

1. Wash hands.
2. Select a plate and plastic knife.
3. Use tongs to place a hot dog on the plate.
4. Cut the hot dog into strips, stopping the cut at the 1" mark, with adult assistance if needed.
5. Turn the hot dog and make another cut. This will also stop at the 1" mark. (These cutting motions are designed to keep the hot dog together. The strips that are cut are not to be separated from the entire hot dog.)
6. Place the cut hot dog in the pan, using the tongs.

The adult will complete the following steps:

1. Boil the hot dogs on the stove. The strips will spread apart and curl upward.
2. Use a colander to drain the hot dogs.
3. Place a hot dog on an individual plate for each child.
4. Serve the hot dogs for lunch or snack.
5. Ask the children, "How has the hot dog changed?"

⊘ SAFETY PRECAUTION:

Observe the children closely when they eat hot dogs, because hot dogs present a choking hazard.

VEGETARIAN SUBSTITUTION:

Use veggie hot dogs. If using some veggie hot dogs and some meat hot dogs, cook them separately. The "legs" on the veggie octopus will not curl like those on the meat octopus; however, they will separate.

GROUP SIZE:

1–4 children

Open-Faced Tuna Bun

AGES: 3–5

DEVELOPMENTAL GOALS:

- ✄ To provide a nutritious snack
- ✄ To develop fine motor skills

LEARNING OBJECTIVE:

The child will participate in measuring, mixing, and spreading the ingredients to make a nutritious snack.

MATERIALS:

Ingredients	Equipment
Water-based tuna	Baking sheet
Mayonnaise	Aluminum foil
Individually wrapped slices of cheese	Permanent marker
Hot dog buns	Bowls
	Spoons for stirring
	Measuring spoons
	Plates
	Knife (for adult use)
	Plastic knives (for children's use)

ADULT PREPARATION:

1. Preheat the oven to 350°.
2. Drain water from the tuna.

continued

Open-Faced Tuna Bun continued

   3. Place the tuna in a bowl.

   4. Put mayonnaise in a bowl.

   5. If hot dog buns are not precut, cut the buns in half lengthwise.

   6. Place a bun half on an individual plate for each child.

   7. Cover baking sheet with foil.

PROCEDURES:

The child will complete the following steps:

1. Wash hands.
2. Measure 2 tablespoons of tuna and put it in a bowl.
3. Measure 1 teaspoon of mayonnaise and add it to the bowl.
4. Stir the two ingredients; mix them well.
5. Choose a plate with a bun.
6. Use a plastic knife to spread the tuna mixture on the bun.
7. Unwrap one slice of cheese.
8. Tear the cheese to fit on top of the bun over the tuna.

The adult will complete the following steps:

1. Place the bun on the foil-covered baking sheet.
2. Write the child's name below the bun with a permanent marker.
3. When the baking sheet is full, place the tuna buns in the oven for approximately 10 minutes.
4. Remove the tuna buns from the oven and allow them to cool slightly.
5. Place each tuna bun on an individual plate.
6. Serve the open-faced tuna buns for lunch or snack.

VEGETARIAN SUBSTITUTION:

Omit the tuna and make an open-faced cheese bun.

GROUP SIZE:

3–5 children

Porcupines

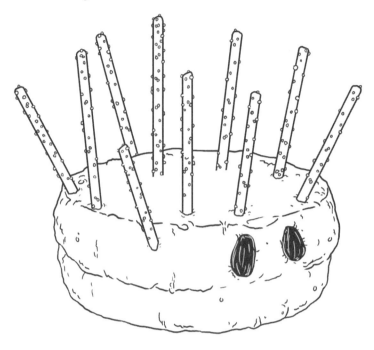

AGES: 3–5

DEVELOPMENTAL GOALS:

✄ To promote rational counting

✄ To develop finger dexterity

LEARNING OBJECTIVE:

The child will count and position pretzels on a biscuit to make a porcupine.

MATERIALS:

Ingredients	Equipment
Canned biscuits (one biscuit per child) Pretzel sticks Raisins	Baking sheet Aluminum foil Permanent marker Wax paper Bowls Spoon Plate

ADULT PREPARATION:

1. Open a can of biscuits, separate the biscuits, and place them on a plate.

2. Pour pretzel sticks in a bowl.

3. Place raisins in a bowl and add a spoon.

continued

Porcupines continued

4. Tear a sheet of wax paper for each child.

5. Cover the baking sheet with foil.

6. Preheat the oven to 350°.

PROCEDURES:

The child will complete the following steps:

1. Wash hands.

2. Take a sheet of wax paper.

3. Take one uncooked biscuit from the plate and place it on his or her sheet of wax paper.

4. Count out 10 pretzel sticks, with adult assistance if needed.

5. Stick the pretzels into the dough in a standing position, to resemble the quills of a porcupine.

6. Use a spoon to count and take two raisins from the bowl and put them into the porcupine biscuit to resemble eyes.

The adult will complete the following steps:

1. Place the porcupine biscuit on the baking sheet.

2. Using a permanent marker, write the child's name on the foil under the biscuit. Place biscuits approximately two inches apart.

3. When the baking sheet is full, bake the biscuits for approximately 10–12 minutes, until the biscuits are golden brown.

⚠ SAFETY PRECAUTION:

Supervise children closely when using raisins, which present a choking hazard.

GROUP SIZE:

3–5 children

Potato Soup

AGES: 3–5

DEVELOPMENTAL GOALS:

✂ To participate in a group project

✂ To promote measurement

LEARNING OBJECTIVE:

The children will measure ingredients as they participate, as a group, in making potato soup.

MATERIALS:

Ingredients	Equipment
Potatoes	Vegetable peeler
Baby carrots	Colander
Vegetable broth	Measuring cups
Milk	Can opener
Shredded cheddar cheese	Pan
Water	Cutting board
	Knife
	Bowls

ADULT PREPARATION:

1. Wash and peel the potatoes.

2. Cut the potatoes into cubes.

3. Rinse the potatoes in a colander and place them in a bowl.

continued

Potato Soup continued

4. Rinse and slice baby carrots.

5. Place the carrots, milk, salt, and cheese in separate bowls.

PROCEDURES:

All children will complete the following steps:

1. Measure and add the following ingredients to the pan:

   a. ¼ cup potatoes

   b. 1 tablespoon carrots

   c. 1 tablespoon shredded cheddar cheese

   d. 2 tablespoons milk

   e. A pinch of salt

The adult will complete the following steps:

1. Open and pour the can of vegetable broth into the pan. Use only the amount needed to cover the vegetables.

2. If necessary, add water to make sure the vegetables are under liquid.

3. Place the pan on the stove and simmer until the vegetables are tender.

4. Serve in bowls for snack or lunch.

Note: If students are present for a longer day, a crockpot may be used to cook the soup.

SAFETY PRECAUTION:

Supervise children closely when using small vegetable pieces, which present a choking hazard.

GROUP SIZE:

3–6 children

Purple Cow

AGES: 3–5

DEVELOPMENTAL GOALS:

- ✄ To participate in a small group activity
- ✄ To practice measuring

LEARNING OBJECTIVE:

The children will take turns measuring and pouring ingredients to make a purple cow.

MATERIALS:

Ingredients	Equipment
Small can of frozen grape juice concentrate 2% milk Vanilla ice cream	Blender Measuring cups Spoons

ADULT PREPARATION:

1. Thaw the can of frozen grape juice.

PROCEDURES:

The children will complete the following steps:

1. Wash hands.

continued

Purple Cow continued

2. Take turns adding the following ingredients to the blender:

    a. 2 cups vanilla ice cream (two children may add 1 cup each)

    b. 1 cup milk (two children may add ½ cup each)

    c. ¾ cup grape juice concentrate (two children may add ⅜ cup each)

3. Blend until all the ingredients are mixed.

Note: This makes ½-cup servings for six or seven children.

GROUP SIZE:

3–6 children

Queen's Tarts

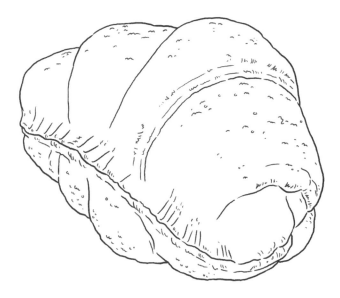

AGES: 3–5

DEVELOPMENTAL GOALS:
- ✂ To observe transformations
- ✂ To stimulate fine motor control

LEARNING OBJECTIVE:
The child will use his or her fine motor skills as he or she puts together a tart and observes the transformation.

MATERIALS:

Ingredients	Equipment
Cherry pie filling Refrigerated cans of crescent rolls	Baking sheet Foil Permanent marker Plates Fork Bowl Tablespoon (measuring spoon) Can opener

ADULT PREPARATION:

1. Cover baking sheet with aluminum foil.
2. Open the can of cherry pie filling and place it in a bowl.
3. Open the can of crescent dough. Separate the crescents and place them on a plate.
4. Preheat the oven to 400°.

continued

Queen's Tarts continued

PROCEDURES:

The child will complete the following steps:

1. Wash hands.
2. Take a plate and place a crescent on the plate.
3. Measure 2 tablespoons of cherry pie filling and place them on the crescent.
4. Place a second crescent roll on top of the cherry pie filling, laying the crescent in the same direction as the first one, matching up the corners and sides.
5. Use a fork to crimp the edges, thus sealing the two crescent rolls together, with adult assistance if needed.

The adult will complete the following steps:

1. Lift the cherry turnover off the plate and onto the foil-covered baking sheet.
2. Write the child's name below the turnover with a permanent marker.
3. When the baking sheet is full, bake at 400° for approximately 10–12 minutes or until golden brown.

SAFETY PRECAUTION:

Supervise children closely when using small food such as cherries that present a choking hazard.

GROUP SIZE:

2–5 children

Quiche

AGES: 3–5

DEVELOPMENTAL GOALS:

✄ To practice cooking procedures

✄ To develop self-help skills

LEARNING OBJECTIVE:

The child will measure and pour to make an individual quiche.

MATERIALS:

Ingredients	Equipment
Quiche mix (found in the frozen foods aisle of the grocery store) Individual pastry shells (also found in the frozen foods aisle)	Baking sheet Measuring cup Permanent marker Child-size pitcher Toothpick

ADULT PREPARATION:

1. Thaw quiche mix in the refrigerator overnight.
2. Write each child's name on the bottom of one of the mini pie pans containing individual pastry shells, with a permanent marker.
3. Pour quiche mix into a child-size pitcher.
4. Preheat the oven to 350°.

PROCEDURES:

The child will complete the following steps:

1. Wash hands.
2. Select the individual pastry shell with his or her name.

continued

Quiche continued

3. Pour ¼ cup quiche into the measuring cup.

4. Pour the quiche mix into the individual pastry shell.

The adult will complete the following steps:

1. Place the quiche on the baking tray.

2. Bake the quiche for 30 minutes or until an inserted toothpick comes out clean.

Note: A 26-ounce container of quiche mix makes 14 servings.

GROUP SIZE:

3–5 children

Quick Crispy Dessert

AGES: 3–5

DEVELOPMENTAL GOALS:

✂ To develop fine motor control

✂ To practice measuring

LEARNING OBJECTIVE:

The child will measure and mix ingredients to make a quick crispy dessert.

MATERIALS:

Ingredients	Equipment
Corn syrup	Measuring spoons
Butter or margarine	Stirring spoons
Can of vanilla frosting	Bowls
Toasted rice cereal	Tray
	Aluminum foil
	Permanent marker

ADULT PREPARATION:

1. Melt butter.

2. Pour the melted butter and corn syrup into separate bowls.

3. Open the can of vanilla frosting.

4. Pour toasted rice cereal into a large bowl.

continued

Quick Crispy Dessert continued

PROCEDURES:

The child will complete the following steps:

1. Wash hands.

2. The child will measure and mix the following ingredients in a bowl.

   a. 1 teaspoon corn syrup

   b. 1 teaspoon melted butter

   c. 2 tablespoons vanilla frosting

3. The child will measure and pour ⅜ cup (5 tablespoons) of toasted rice cereal into the bowl, and mix well, covering the cereal with the first three ingredients.

4. The child will spoon the mixture onto the foil-covered tray.

The adult will complete the following steps:

1. Write the child's name below the quick crispy dessert.

2. Refrigerate the dessert for approximately 30 minutes, until firm.

Note: The 16-ounce container of frosting makes 12 servings.

GROUP SIZE:

3–4 children

Radish Sandwich

AGES: 3–5

DEVELOPMENTAL GOALS:

✂ To stimulate eye-hand coordination

✂ To develop fine motor skills

LEARNING OBJECTIVE:

The child will use a knife to spread butter and will layer radishes on a sandwich.

MATERIALS:

Ingredients	Equipment
Sliced bread (one slice per child) Radishes (approximately two per child) 8-ounce tub of soft butter or margarine	Plates Plastic knives Paring knife Cutting board Bowl

ADULT PREPARATION:

1. Slice radishes ⅛" to ¼" thick and place them in a bowl.
2. Cut bread slices in half; put two halves on each child's plate.

continued

Radish Sandwich continued

PROCEDURES:

The child will complete the following steps:

1. Wash hands.
2. Use a plastic knife to spread butter on each bread half.
3. Layer radish slices on one half piece of buttered bread.
4. Top the radishes with the other half slice of buttered bread.

GROUP SIZE:

2–4 children

Raisin Oatmeal Cookie

AGES: 4–5

DEVELOPMENTAL GOALS:

✂ To participate in a large group activity

✂ To promote social development through taking turns

LEARNING OBJECTIVE:

The children will participate in a large group activity by taking turns measuring and mixing ingredients as they make raisin oatmeal cookies.

MATERIALS:

Ingredients	Equipment
Box of white cake mix	Mixing bowl
8 ounces whipped topping	Stirring spoon
2 eggs	Measuring cups
Vanilla	Measuring spoon
Raisins	Baking sheets
Quick-cooking oats	Aluminum foil

ADULT PREPARATION:

1. Preheat the oven to 350°.
2. Cover the baking sheets with aluminum foil.

continued

Raisin Oatmeal Cookie continued

PROCEDURES:

The children will complete the following steps:

1. Wash hands.
2. Take turns to measure, add, and mix the following ingredients:
   a. 1 box cake mix
   b. 8 ounces whipped topping
   c. 2 eggs
   d. ¼ teaspoon vanilla
   e. 1 cup of raisins
   f. 1 cup of quick-cooking oats
3. When all the ingredients are mixed, take turns using a small melon baller to place the dough on the baking sheets, putting the scoops approximately one to two inches apart.

The adult will complete the following step:

1. Place the cookies in the oven for approximately 15–20 minutes, depending on the size of the cookies. The cookies are golden brown when completely baked.

Note: Raisin oatmeal bars may be made in place of cookies by spreading the dough in a 9" by 13" greased pan. Bake for approximately 25–30 minutes or until golden brown.

SAFETY PRECAUTION:

Supervise children closely when using raisins, which present a choking hazard.

GROUP SIZE:

6–12 children

Root Beer Float

AGES: 2–5

DEVELOPMENTAL GOALS:

- ✂ To promote pouring ability
- ✂ To make predictions

LEARNING OBJECTIVE:

The child will practice pouring and adding ingredients as he or she predicts the outcome of making a root beer float.

MATERIALS:

Ingredients	Equipment
Root beer Vanilla ice cream	10-ounce clear plastic cups Permanent marker Small ice cream scoop Child-size pitcher

ADULT PREPARATION:

1. Soften ice cream by putting it in the refrigerator for approximately 20 minutes before using.

2. Using a permanent marker, draw a line around each plastic cup, about halfway between the bottom and the top.

3. Pour root beer into a child-size pitcher.

continued

109

Root Beer Float continued

PROCEDURES:

The child will complete the following steps:

1. Wash hands.
2. Use the child-size pitcher to pour root beer into his or her cup, stopping at the line drawn around each cup.
3. Answer the question, "What will happen when ice cream is put into the root beer?"
4. Use the ice cream scoop to place ice cream in the root beer.
5. Describe the reaction between the root beer and the ice cream.

GROUP SIZE:

3–5 children

Sautéed Spinach

AGES: 3–5

DEVELOPMENTAL GOALS:

- ✂ To introduce new foods
- ✂ To measure varying amounts

LEARNING OBJECTIVE:

The child will be introduced to a new food while he or she measures ingredients to make sautéed spinach.

MATERIALS:

Ingredients	Equipment
20 ounces frozen spinach (makes eight servings) Minced garlic (found in the refrigerated section of the grocery store, in a jar) Olive oil Salt	Electric skillet 2-quart microwave dish Fork ¼-cup measure Measuring spoons Wooden spoon Colander Bowls Plates Tape

ADULT PREPARATION:

1. Place frozen spinach in a microwavable dish.
2. Cook the spinach in the microwave for approximately 8–10 minutes on high.

continued

Sautéed Spinach continued

3. Using the colander, drain the excess liquid from the spinach.
4. Place the spinach in a bowl.
5. Place the salt, olive oil, and minced garlic in separate bowls.
6. Roll towels and place them around the electric skillet.
7. Tape the cord to the table and floor.

PROCEDURES:

The child will complete the following steps:

1. Measure 1 teaspoon of olive oil and put it in the skillet.
2. Measure ¼ teaspoon of minced garlic and add it to the skillet.
3. Use the fork to pick up the spinach and fill the ¼-cup measure.
4. Add the spinach to the skillet.
5. Add a pinch of salt to the skillet.
6. Stir the mixture with a wooden spoon, with adult help if needed.

The adult will complete the following step:

1. Spoon the mixture onto a plate when it is heated thoroughly.

Note: The ingredients given are for one child. If additional children cook at the same time, they take turns measuring out their own ingredients. All their ingredients are combined together in the skillet.

SUBSTITUTION:

If minced garlic is not available, finely chopped fresh garlic may be used.

SAFETY PRECAUTION:

Supervise children closely when using cooking appliances in the classroom. As an alternative, all children may take turns adding their own ingredients to a skillet; then the adult may take the pan into the kitchen to cook.

GROUP SIZE:

1–4 children

Scalloped Potatoes

AGES: 3–5

DEVELOPMENTAL GOALS:

✂ To make a nutritious snack

✂ To practice measuring

LEARNING OBJECTIVE:

The child will measure ingredients as he or she makes scalloped potatoes, a nutritious snack.

MATERIALS:

Ingredients	Equipment
Potatoes Milk Shredded cheddar cheese Sliced ham (optional)	Vegetable peeler Bowls Knife Cutting board Muffin tin Foil muffin liners Measuring spoons ¼-cup measure Permanent marker

ADULT PREPARATION:

1. Preheat the oven to 350°.
2. Wash, peel, and cut the potatoes into ½" cubes.
3. Put the potato cubes in a bowl.

continued

Scalloped Potatoes continued

4. If using ham, chop the ham into small pieces and place in a separate bowl.

5. Place milk and shredded cheddar cheese in separate bowls.

6. Write children's names on the bottoms of foil muffin liners.

PROCEDURES:

The child will complete the following steps:

1. Wash hands.

2. Select the muffin liner with his or her name on the bottom.

3. Measure and put the following ingredients into the liner:

   a. ¼ cup potatoes

   b. 1 teaspoon ham (optional)

   c. 1 tablespoon shredded cheese

   d. 1 tablespoon milk

The adult will complete the following steps:

1. Place the foil liner in the muffin pan.

2. When the muffin pan is full, bake the scalloped potatoes for 20 minutes, or until the potatoes are tender.

GROUP SIZE:

3–5 children

Starfish

AGES: 3–5

DEVELOPMENTAL GOALS:

- ✂ To recognize the star shape
- ✂ To promote self-help skills

LEARNING OBJECTIVE:

The child will make his or her own snack in the shape of a star, as they create a starfish.

MATERIALS:

Ingredients	Equipment
White or wheat bread Peanut butter Toasted whole grain oat cereal	Plates Star cookie cutters Plastic knives Resealable plastic bags Child-size rolling pins Bowls Tablespoon (measuring) Picture of a starfish Permanent marker

ADULT PREPARATION:

1. Write children's names on individual paper plates.
2. Place toasted whole grain oat cereal and peanut butter in separate bowls.

continued

Starfish continued

PROCEDURES:

The child will complete the following steps:

1. Wash hands.
2. Look at a picture of a starfish.
3. Describe the picture of the starfish. Answer the questions, "What shape do you see? How does the starfish feel? Smooth or rough?"
4. Select the plate and a piece of bread.
5. Use a star cookie cutter and press a star shape in the bread.
6. Put the bread scraps in a bowl; leave the star-shaped bread on the plate.
7. Spread peanut butter on the star-shaped bread using a plastic knife.
8. Measure 1–2 tablespoons of toasted whole grain oat cereal and place it in a resealable plastic bag.
9. Remove the air from the bag and seal it, with adult help if necessary.
10. Use the rolling pin to crush the oats inside the bag.
11. Open the resealable bag and sprinkle the crushed cereal onto the peanut-butter-covered star.

Notes: Use the bread scraps to feed the birds. If children are allergic to peanut butter, use honey as a substitute.

GROUP SIZE:

3–5 children

Tortilla Chips

AGES: 3–5

DEVELOPMENTAL GOALS:

✂ To promote the use of a knife

✂ To enhance eye-hand coordination

LEARNING OBJECTIVE:

The child will practice cutting with a knife while making tortilla chips.

MATERIALS:

Ingredients	Equipment
Flour tortillas	Baking sheets Aluminum foil Permanent marker Plates Knife Cutting board Plastic knives

ADULT PREPARATION:

1. Preheat the oven to 350°.
2. Cut flour tortillas in half.
3. Cover baking sheet with foil.

PROCEDURES:

The child will complete the following steps:

1. Wash hands.
2. Place half a flour tortilla on a plate.

continued

Tortilla Chips continued

3. Use a plastic knife and cut the tortilla into smaller pieces.

4. Place the tortilla pieces on the baking sheet covered with foil.

The adult will complete the following steps:

1. Write the child's name below his or her tortilla pieces.

2. Once the baking sheet is full, bake the tortilla pieces for approximately 10 minutes, until they are crisp and golden brown.

3. Allow the chips to cool slightly, and then serve with salsa for a snack.

GROUP SIZE:

1–6 children

Trail Mix

AGES: 3–5

DEVELOPMENTAL GOALS:
- ✂ To practice measuring
- ✂ To follow directions

LEARNING OBJECTIVE:

The child will follow directions measuring and adding ingredients to make trail mix.

MATERIALS:

Ingredients	Equipment
Toasted whole grain oat cereal Small pretzels Raisins Candy-coated chocolate pieces	Tablespoon (measuring) ¼-cup measure Resealable plastic bag (sandwich size) Permanent marker Bowls

ADULT PREPARATION:

1. Write the children's names on individual resealable plastic bags with a permanent marker.
2. Place cereal, pretzels, raisins, and candy in individual bowls.

continued

Trail Mix continued

PROCEDURES:

The child will complete the following steps:

1. Wash hands.
2. Select the resealable plastic bag with his or her name.
3. Measure and add the following ingredients to his or her plastic bag:
   a. 2 tablespoons toasted whole grain oat cereal
   b. ¼ cup pretzels
   c. 2 tablespoons raisins
   d. 1 tablespoon candy-coated chocolate pieces
4. Seal the bag, with adult assistance if necessary.
5. Shake his or her bag until the ingredients are thoroughly mixed.

SAFETY PRECAUTION:

Supervise children closely when working with small foods that present a choking hazard.

GROUP SIZE:

3–5 children

Turkeys

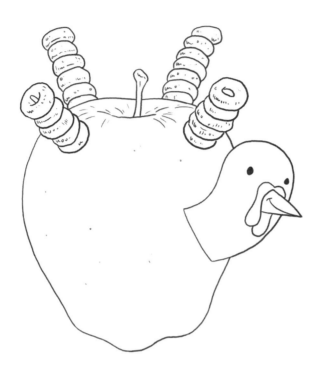

AGES: 3–5

DEVELOPMENTAL GOALS:

✄ To promote fine motor control

✄ To develop eye-hand coordination

LEARNING OBJECTIVE:

The child will utilize eye-hand coordination and fine motor control while placing toothpicks and cereal on an apple to make a turkey.

MATERIALS:

Ingredients	Equipment
Apples (one for each child) Toasted whole grain oat cereal	Party-style toothpicks (thicker than regular toothpicks) Bowls Plates Construction paper Turkey head pattern Pencil Scissors

ADULT PREPARATION:

1. Wash apples.
2. Using a turkey head pattern, construction paper, pencil, and scissors, make a construction paper turkey head for each child.
3. Put cereal and toothpicks in separate bowls.

continued

Turkeys continued

PROCEDURES:

The child will complete the following steps:

1. Wash hands.
2. Select a plate and an apple.
3. Set the apple on the plate.
4. Select four or five toothpicks.
5. Stick the toothpicks into the top of the apple.
6. Fill each toothpick with toasted whole grain oat cereal.
7. Attach the turkey head on one side of the apple, with toothpicks, using adult assistance if needed.

Note: The turkey may be used as a Thanksgiving centerpiece.

You may choose to put four toothpicks on the bottom of the apple for legs, to make it look as though the turkey is standing.

⚠ SAFETY PRECAUTION:

Supervise children closely when using small food and toothpicks, as these present choking hazards.

GROUP SIZE:

3–5 children

Ugly Bugs

AGES: 3–5

DEVELOPMENTAL GOALS:

- ✂ To promote creativity
- ✂ To observe a transformation

LEARNING OBJECTIVE:

The child will observe a transformation of dough into a cooked product while creating ugly bugs.

MATERIALS:

Ingredients	Equipment
Canned biscuits	Baking sheet
Small pretzel twists	Aluminum foil
Raisins	Permanent marker
Slivered almonds	Bowls
Candy sprinkles (found in baking aisle of the grocery store)	Plates
	Knife

ADULT PREPARATION:

1. Cover baking sheet with aluminum foil.
2. Place pretzels, raisins, sprinkles, and almonds in separate bowls.
3. Open the canned biscuits and separate the dough, placing the biscuits on a plate.
4. Preheat the oven to 400°.

continued

Ugly Bugs continued

PROCEDURES:

The child will complete the following steps:

1. Wash hands.
2. Place a section of bread dough on a plate.
3. Form and decorate the dough into an ugly bug. Raisins may be used for eyes, slivered almonds for scales, pretzels for wings, and sprinkles for color.

The adult will complete the following steps:

1. Place the bug on the foil-covered baking sheet.
2. Write the child's name below his or her bug with a permanent marker.
3. When the baking sheet is full, bake the bugs for approximately 10–12 minutes.

Note: If a child has nut allergies, omit the almonds.

SAFETY PRECAUTION:

Supervise children closely when working with small foods that present a choking hazard.

GROUP SIZE:

3–5 children

Upside-Down Cake

AGES: 2½–5

DEVELOPMENTAL GOALS:
✄ To follow directions
✄ To sequence objects

LEARNING OBJECTIVE:
The child will follow directions while sequencing ingredients to make an upside-down cake.

MATERIALS:

Ingredients	Equipment
White cake mix	Colander
Eggs	Foil muffin liners
Vegetable oil	Mixing bowl
Water	Electric mixer or egg beater
Brown sugar	Baking sheet or muffin tin
Crushed pineapple	Permanent marker
	Measuring spoons
	Toothpick

ADULT PREPARATION:

1. Preheat the oven to 350°.
2. Write children's names on the bottoms of the foil liners with a permanent marker.

continued

125

Upside-Down Cake continued

3. If the foil liners have paper inserts, remove the paper and set it aside.
4. Drain the juice from the crushed pineapple by putting it in a colander.
5. Place pineapple and brown sugar in separate bowls.
6. Mix the cake batter by following the directions on the box, but do not bake it.

PROCEDURES:

The child will complete the following steps:

1. Wash hands.
2. Select the muffin liner with his or her name on the bottom.
3. Measure 2 teaspoons of brown sugar into the foil liner.
4. Measure and add 1 tablespoon of crushed pineapple to the foil liner.
5. Measure and add 3 or 4 tablespoons of cake batter to the liner, leaving approximately ¼" to ½" of space at the top of the liner.

The adult will complete the following steps:

1. Place the upside-down cake batter on a baking sheet or muffin tin.
2. Once the tray is full, bake the cakes for approximately 25 minutes. A toothpick inserted halfway into the cake should come out clean. Avoid pushing the toothpick in too far, or the topping at the bottom will remain on the toothpick.
3. Allow the cakes to cool.
4. Give each child their cake on a plate.

The child will complete the following step:

1. Turn the cake upside down and remove the foil liner. The ingredients that were on the bottom of the liner are now the topping.

Note: The children may help mix the cake batter.

GROUP SIZE:

3–5 children

U.S. Flag

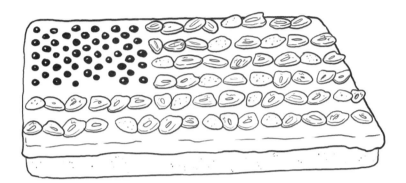

AGES: 3–5

DEVELOPMENTAL GOALS:

✂ To practice counting

✂ To recognize colors

LEARNING OBJECTIVE:

The children will practice color recognition and counting while making the U.S. flag.

MATERIALS:

Ingredients	Equipment
White cake mix	Mixing bowl
Eggs	Electric mixer or egg beater
Oil	9" × 13" baking pan
Water	Spatula
Strawberries	Spoons
Blueberries	Cutting board
Whipped topping in	Knife
plastic container	Bowls
	U.S. Flag

ADULT PREPARATION:

1. Follow the directions on the cake mix to make the cake, one day before the children take part in this cake-decorating activity.
2. On the day of the activity, wash and slice the strawberries and put them in a bowl.
3. Wash the blueberries and put them in a separate bowl.

PROCEDURES:

The children will complete the following steps:

1. Wash hands.
2. Look at the U.S. flag.

continued

U.S. Flag continued

3. Take turns spreading the whipped topping on the cake with a spatula.

4. Count out 50 blueberries, using a spoon to move the blueberries into a separate bowl as they are counted.

5. Note where the blue area on the flag is located.

6. Take turns spooning the blueberries into the left top corner of the cake.

7. Identify the colors of the stripes on the flag.

8. Take turns spooning the sliced strawberries on the cake to make the red stripes on the flag. Leave room between the rows for the whipped topping to show through (making the white stripes).

Note: It is not possible to place all seven red stripes on the cake.

SAFETY PRECAUTION:

Supervise children closely when using small foods that present a choking hazard.

GROUP SIZE:

6–10 children

Vanilla Pudding

AGES: 2–5

DEVELOPMENTAL GOALS:

- ✂ To coordinate large and small muscles
- ✂ To observe a transformation

LEARNING OBJECTIVE:

The child will measure, pour, and shake ingredients while observing the transformation of ingredients into vanilla pudding.

MATERIALS:

Ingredients	Equipment
Instant vanilla pudding mix Milk	Plastic cups with lids Measuring spoons ½-cup measure Bowls Masking tape Permanent marker

ADULT PREPARATION:

1. Put the milk and instant pudding mix into separate bowls.

continued

Vanilla Pudding continued

PROCEDURES:

The child will complete the following steps:

1. Wash hands.
2. Measure the following ingredients and put them into the plastic cup:
   a. 2 tablespoons pudding mix
   b. ½ cup milk
3. Put the lid securely on the cup, with adult assistance if needed.
4. Shake the cup until the ingredients are thoroughly mixed.

The adult will complete the following steps:

1. Place masking tape on the cup and write the child's name on the cup.
2. Place the cup in the refrigerator until snack time.

Note: The large box (4⅝ ounces) makes six servings.

GROUP SIZE:

2–5 children

Vanilla Wafer Pudding

AGES: 2–5

DEVELOPMENTAL GOALS:

✄ To follow directions

✄ To practice patterning

LEARNING OBJECTIVE:

The child will practice making a pattern by following directions to make vanilla wafer pudding.

MATERIALS:

Ingredients	Equipment
Instant vanilla pudding mix Milk Vanilla wafers Miniature chocolate chips	Bowl to mix pudding Measuring cup Bowls Custard cups, foil muffin liners, or 5-ounce disposable cups Spoons Masking tape Permanent marker

ADULT PREPARATION:

1. Write children's names on masking tape with a permanent marker. Place the masking tape on the custard cups. If custard cups are not available, use foil muffin liners or 5-ounce disposable cups. Names may be written directly on the bottom of liners or disposable cups with a permanent marker. (If using foil liners, remove the interior paper liners and discard.)

continued

Vanilla Wafer Pudding continued

2. Mix the vanilla pudding according to the package directions and set it in the refrigerator until needed.

3. Put the vanilla wafers and miniature chocolate chips in separate bowls.

PROCEDURES:

The child will complete the following steps:

1. Wash hands.

2. Create the following layers in the custard cup:

   a. One vanilla wafer

   b. Vanilla pudding

   c. One vanilla wafer

   d. Vanilla pudding

3. Add miniature chocolate chips to the top layer of pudding.

SAFETY PRECAUTION:

Supervise children closely when using small foods that present a choking hazard.

GROUP SIZE:

2–5 children

Veggie Loaf Cups

AGES: 3–5

DEVELOPMENTAL GOALS:

- ✂ To introduce new foods
- ✂ To sample alternative products

LEARNING OBJECTIVE:

The child will measure and stir ingredients to make a new food (veggie loaf cups).

MATERIALS:

Ingredients	Equipment
Meatless ground burger	Muffin tin
Egg substitute	Foil muffin liners
Italian bread crumbs	Permanent marker
Onion (optional)	Bowls
	Measuring spoons
	Stirring spoons
	Cutting board
	Knife
	Toothpicks

continued

Veggie Loaf Cups continued

ADULT PREPARATION:

1. Preheat oven to 350°.
2. Optional: Wash, peel, and chop an onion into fine pieces.
3. Put onion (optional), egg substitute, meatless ground burger, and Italian bread crumbs into separate bowls.
4. Remove the paper separators from the foil muffin cups and discard them.
5. Write each child's name on the bottom of a foil cup, with a permanent marker.

PROCEDURES:

The child will complete the following steps:

1. Wash hands.
2. Measure the following ingredients and put them in a bowl.
   a. 3 tablespoons meatless ground burger
   b. Optional: ¼ teaspoon to 1 teaspoon chopped onion
   c. 2 tablespoons egg substitute
   d. 1 tablespoon Italian bread crumbs
3. Stir all ingredients well.
4. Select the muffin liner with his or her name.
5. Spoon the mixture into a foil muffin liner, with adult assistance if needed.
6. Press the ingredients down into the liner, with the spoon.

The adult will complete the following steps:

1. Place the foil liner in the muffin tin.
2. When the muffin tin is full, bake the veggie cups for approximately 20 minutes.
3. Stick a toothpick in the loaf cup to test for doneness. When the toothpick comes out clean, the veggie loaf cups are ready.

GROUP SIZE:

3–5 children

Waffle Sandwich

DEVELOPMENTAL GOALS:

✂ To promote social development

✂ To develop fine motor skills

LEARNING OBJECTIVE:

The children will participate in a group cooking experience as they make waffle sandwiches.

MATERIALS:

Ingredients	Equipment
Frozen waffles Natural applesauce	Baking sheet Plates Plastic knives Spoons Small bowls

ADULT PREPARATION:

1. Preheat oven to 350°.

2. Layer baking sheet with frozen waffles.

3. Bake for approximately 10 minutes.

continued

Waffle Sandwich continued

4. Put a waffle on an individual plate for each child.

5. Put applesauce in a small bowl for each child.

PROCEDURES:

The children will complete the following steps:

1. Wash hands.

2. Use a knife to spread applesauce on the waffle.

3. Fold the waffle in half.

4. Pick up the waffle sandwich and eat it.

5. Use a spoon to eat the remainder of the applesauce.

GROUP SIZE:

3–20 children

Watermelon Salad

DEVELOPMENTAL GOALS:

- ✂ To enhance eye-hand coordination
- ✂ To develop counting skills

LEARNING OBJECTIVE:

The child will utilize eye-hand coordination by scooping and counting while making watermelon salad.

MATERIALS:

Ingredients	Equipment
Small seedless watermelon Blueberries Green grapes	Bowls Melon baller Knife Masking tape Permanent marker

ADULT PREPARATION:

1. Wash the outside of the watermelon.
2. Cut the melon in half.
3. Wash the blueberries and green grapes and put them in separate bowls.
4. Cut grapes in half.
5. Using a permanent marker, write the children's names on pieces of masking tape. Place the tape on individual bowls.

continued

Watermelon Salad continued

PROCEDURES:

The child will complete the following steps:

1. Wash hands.
2. Select the bowl with his or her name.
3. Scoop out five balls of watermelon, using the melon baller, and place them in the bowl.
4. Count 10 blueberries and put them in the bowl.
5. Count 5–10 grapes and add them to the bowl.

The adult will complete the following step:

1. Refrigerate the watermelon salad until snack time.

⚠ SAFETY PRECAUTION:

Supervise children closely when using small foods, which present a choking hazard.

GROUP SIZE:

3–5 children

White Clouds

AGES: 2–5

DEVELOPMENTAL GOALS:

✂ To follow directions

✂ To develop listening skills

LEARNING OBJECTIVE:

The child will listen to a story and follow directions to make white clouds.

MATERIALS:

Ingredients	Equipment
Whipped topping	Spoons Tray Wax paper Permanent marker *It Looks Like Spilt Milk* by C. G. Shaw (New York: HarperCollins, 1947)

ADULT PREPARATION:

1. Thaw whipped topping in the refrigerator overnight.
2. Tear wax paper into pieces for each child.
3. Write the child's name on the paper with a permanent marker.

continued

White Clouds continued

PROCEDURES:

The adult will complete the following steps:

1. Read *It Looks Like Spilt Milk*. Clouds resemble spilled milk and other imaginative designs in this children's classic.
2. Ask the children, "What do clouds look like?"

The child will complete the following steps:

1. Wash hands.
2. Select the piece of wax paper with his or her name.
3. Place whipped topping on the wax paper, with spoons.
4. Arrange the topping into different shapes resembling clouds, with their spoons.

The adult will complete the following step:

1. Put the pieces of wax paper containing the clouds on a tray. When the tray is full, the clouds may be put into the freezer until frozen hard.

GROUP SIZE:

2–5 children

X Marks the Spot

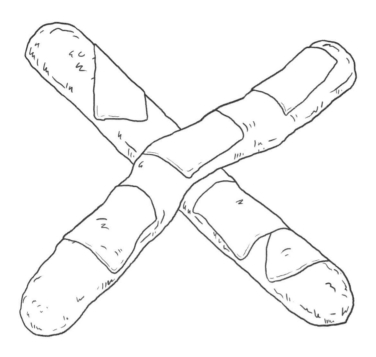

AGES: 3–5

DEVELOPMENTAL GOALS:

✄ To recognize the letter *X*

✄ To promote fine motor control

LEARNING OBJECTIVE:

The child will use fine motor skills to create and then recognize his or her own X marks the spot snack.

MATERIALS:

Ingredients	Equipment
Refrigerated bread stick dough (two sticks per child; usually comes 12 sticks to a can) Individually wrapped cheese slices (one per child)	Baking sheet Permanent marker Knife Paper plates Aluminum foil Plastic knife

ADULT PREPARATION:

1. Remove the pieces of bread stick dough and place them on a plate (two for each child).

2. Place the individually wrapped cheese slices on a separate plate.

3. Tear off a sheet of aluminum foil for each child.

continued

X Marks the Spot continued

4. Draw an *X* on each sheet of aluminum foil, using the dull side of a plastic knife (this will not tear the foil).

5. Preheat the oven to 375°.

PROCEDURES:

The child will complete the following steps:

1. Wash hands.
2. Select a sheet of aluminum foil.
3. Identify the letter written on the foil.
4. Select two strips of bread dough.
5. Lay the strips of dough across the *X* on the foil.
6. Unwrap a slice of cheese and discard the plastic.
7. Tear the cheese into pieces and lay it on top of the bread dough.

The adult will complete the following steps:

1. Lift the aluminum sheet and put it on the baking sheet.
2. Write the child's name on the aluminum foil with a permanent marker.
3. When the baking sheet is full, bake the *X*s for approximately 10–15 minutes.

Note: Sliced bread may be cut into 1" strips to use in place of refrigerated bread stick dough. Broil these *X*s until the cheese has melted.

GROUP SIZE:

3–5 children

Yankee Pot Roast

AGES: 3–5

DEVELOPMENTAL GOALS:

- ✄ To promote nutrition
- ✄ To develop fine motor skills

LEARNING OBJECTIVE:

The child will select and place ingredients in individual muffin liners to make a nutritious Yankee pot roast.

MATERIALS:

Ingredients	Equipment
Beef stew meat	Muffin tin
Carrots	Foil muffin liners
Potatoes	Cutting board
Jar of ready-made gravy	Knife
Water	Vegetable peeler
	Tablespoons (measuring)
	Bowls
	2 pots to boil ingredients
	Aluminum foil
	Permanent marker

ADULT PREPARATION:

1. Preheat the oven to 350°.
2. Write children's names on individual foil muffin liners.
3. Remove the paper separators from the foil liners and discard.
4. Wash and cut carrots into small chunks.
5. Wash, peel, and cut potatoes into ½" cubes.
6. Boil vegetables until tender.
7. Cut stew meat into bite-size pieces.
8. Boil stew meat in a separate pot until thoroughly cooked.
9. Put the vegetables, stew meat, and gravy into separate bowls.

continued

Yankee Pot Roast continued

PROCEDURES:

The child will complete the following steps:

1. Wash hands.
2. Select the foil liner with his or her name.
3. Measure and place in the muffin liner the following ingredients, in this order:
   a. 1 tablespoon of meat
   b. 2 tablespoons of vegetables
   c. 1 tablespoon of gravy

The adult will complete the following steps:

1. Place the foil muffin liner into the muffin tin.
2. Once the tin is full, cover the entire tin with foil and place it in the oven for 10–15 minutes, until the food is thoroughly warmed.

Note: Be sure each child puts both carrots and potatoes into the yankee pot roast. Provide extra gravy if desired when the pot roast is served.

VEGETARIAN SUBSTITUTION:

Use meatless ground burger and cream of mushroom soup in place of the beef and gravy.

GROUP SIZE:

3–5 children

Yogurt Dip

AGES: 3–5

DEVELOPMENTAL GOALS:

- ✂ To create a healthy snack
- ✂ To promote fine muscle development

LEARNING OBJECTIVE:

The child will use fine muscles to measure and stir ingredients while making a healthy snack.

MATERIALS:

Ingredients	Equipment

Flavored fruit yogurt
Whipped cream cheese
Vanilla
Suggested fruit to dip:
  strawberries, bananas,
  or apples
	Custard cups or 5-ounce disposable
	  cups
	Measuring spoons
	Stirring spoons
	Permanent marker
	Masking tape
	Tray
	Bowls

ADULT PREPARATION:

1. Put flavored yogurt, whipped cream cheese, and vanilla into separate bowls.
2. Write each child's name with a permanent marker on a piece of masking tape; place the masking tape on the child's cup.

continued

Yogurt Dip continued

PROCEDURES:

The child will complete the following steps:

1. Wash hands.
2. Select the cup with his or her name.
3. Measure the following ingredients into the cup and mix them well with a spoon:
   a. 1 tablespoon yogurt
   b. 1 tablespoon whipped cream cheese
   c. ⅛ teaspoon of vanilla
4. Place the yogurt dip on a tray.

The adult will complete the following steps:

1. Refrigerate the dip until snack time.
2. Serve the dip with cut fruit such as strawberries, bananas, or apples.

SAFETY PRECAUTION:

Supervise children closely when using small pieces of fruit, which present a choking hazard.

GROUP SIZE:

3–5 children

Yummy Yams

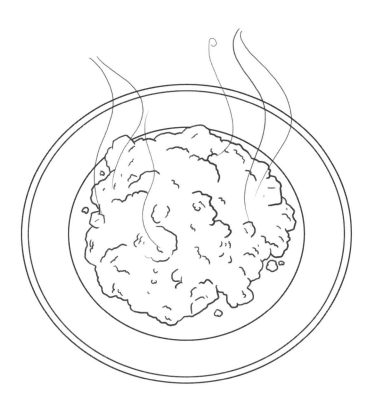

AGES: 3–5

DEVELOPMENTAL GOALS:

- ✂ To stimulate eye-hand coordination
- ✂ To promote measurement

LEARNING OBJECTIVE:

The child will slice and measure ingredients to make yummy yams.

MATERIALS:

Ingredients	Equipment
15-ounce can of yams (serves 5–6) Ground cinnamon Tub of soft butter or margarine Lite pancake syrup	Can opener Colander Foil muffin liners Muffin tin or baking sheet Permanent marker Large bowl Small bowls Potato masher Measuring cup and spoons Spoon

continued

147

Yummy Yams continued

ADULT PREPARATION:

1. Preheat the oven to 350°.
2. Using a permanent marker, write the children's names on the bottoms of the foil muffin liners.
3. Open the can of yams, use a colander to drain the liquid, and place the yams in a large bowl.
4. Use a potato masher to mash the yams.
5. Put the cinnamon in a small bowl.
6. Pour lite syrup into another bowl.

PROCEDURES:

The child will complete the following steps:

1. Wash hands.
2. Use a spoon to place mashed yams in a measuring cup.
3. Place ¼ cup of yams in a separate bowl.
4. Measure ¼ teaspoon of cinnamon and put it on top of the yams.
5. Measure 1 teaspoon of butter or margarine and put it on top of the cinnamon.
6. Stir all ingredients until completely blended.
7. Spoon the mixture into the foil muffin liner.
8. Measure 1 tablespoon of lite pancake syrup and pour it over the yams.

The adult will complete the following steps:

1. Place the muffin liner on a baking sheet or muffin tin.
2. Once the baking sheet or muffin tin is full, bake the yams in the oven for 15 minutes.

GROUP SIZE:

3–4 children

148

Zebra Pudding

AGES: 3–5

DEVELOPMENTAL GOALS:

- ✂ To practice patterning
- ✂ To follow directions

LEARNING OBJECTIVE:

The child will pattern pudding by following directions to make zebra pudding.

MATERIALS:

Ingredients	Equipment
Instant vanilla pudding mix Instant chocolate pudding mix Milk	Picture of a zebra Clear cups Spoons Mixing bowls Measuring cups Masking tape Permanent marker Tray

ADULT PREPARATION:

1. Make chocolate and vanilla pudding separately according to package directions.
2. Chill the pudding until needed.

continued

Zebra Pudding continued

3. Write the children's names on masking tape with the permanent marker.

4. Put the masking tape on clear cups.

PROCEDURES:

The child will complete the following steps:

1. Wash hands.

2. Look at a picture of a zebra.

3. Identify the colors of the stripes on the zebra.

4. Select the cup with his or her name.

5. Spoon chocolate and vanilla pudding into the cup in alternating layers.

The adult will complete the following step:

1. Refrigerate the pudding until snack time.

GROUP SIZE:

3–5 children

Zesty Popcorn

AGES: 4–5

DEVELOPMENTAL GOALS:

- ✂ To promote measurement skills
- ✂ To develop fine motor skills

LEARNING OBJECTIVE:

The child will measure and shake ingredients to make zesty popcorn.

MATERIALS:

Ingredients	Equipment
Package of microwave popcorn (makes 6–7 servings) Seasoned salt	Measuring cup ¼ teaspoon measuring spoon Quart-size resealable plastic bag Large bowl Small bowl

ADULT PREPARATION:

1. Make popcorn according to package directions and pour into a large bowl.
2. Put the seasoned salt into a separate small bowl.

continued

Zesty Popcorn continued

PROCEDURES:

The child will complete the following steps:

1. Wash hands.
2. Measure 1 cup popcorn and put it into the plastic resealable bag.
3. Measure ¼ teaspoon seasoned salt and place it in the bag with the popcorn.
4. Seal the bag.
5. Shake the bag until the seasoning is mixed with the popcorn.

ⓘ SAFETY PRECAUTION:

Supervise children closely when using popcorn, which is a choking hazard.

GROUP SIZE:

3–4 children

Zucchini Muffins

AGES: 3–5

DEVELOPMENTAL GOALS:

✄ To observe a transformation

✄ To enhance self-help skills

LEARNING OBJECTIVE:

The child will observe a transformation of batter into baked goods while making a zucchini muffin.

MATERIALS:

Ingredients	Equipment
Cinnamon muffin mix Egg Milk Zucchini	Mixing bowl Measuring cups Stirring spoon Colander Vegetable peeler Grater Bowls Foil muffin liners Muffin tin or baking sheet Permanent marker Toothpick

continued

Zucchini Muffins continued

ADULT PREPARATION:

1. Peel and grate zucchini.
2. Place the grated zucchini in a colander to dry.
3. Write children's names on the bottoms of foil liners with a permanent marker.
4. Mix the muffin batter according to directions. Set aside.
5. Preheat the oven to 400°.

PROCEDURES:

The child will complete the following steps:

1. Wash hands.
2. Measure and place the following ingredients in a bowl:
   a. 3 tablespoons muffin batter
   b. 1 tablespoon grated zucchini
3. Carefully stir the zucchini into the batter.
4. Select the muffin liner with his or her name on the bottom.
5. Spoon the batter into the liner, with adult help if needed.

The adult will complete the following steps:

1. Place the foil liner on a baking sheet or in a muffin tin.
2. When the baking sheet or muffin tin is full, bake the muffins for 20–25 minutes, until a toothpick inserted into a muffin comes out clean.

GROUP SIZE:

3–5 children

154

References

Herr, J. (2002). *Working with young children.* Tinley Park, IL: Goodheart-Willcox.

Hise, P. (2004, April). Orange alert: Protect yourself from foodborne illness. *Vegetarian Times, 320,* 79–83.

Shaw, C. G. (1947). *It looks like spilt milk.* New York: HarperCollins.

Squires, S. (2004, October 19). 10 ways to fight childhood obesity. *The Detroit News.* Retrieved February 4, 2005, from <http://www.detnews.com/2004/lifestyle/0410/19/f08-307451.htm>.

Appendix A: Common Measurement Equivalents

Cups	Ounces	Tablespoons	Combination	Teaspoons
¹⁄₁₆	½	1		3
¹⁄₁₂			1 tbsp. + 1 tsp.	4
⅛	1	2		6
⅙			2 tbsp. + 2 tsp.	8
¼	2	4	¼ c.	12
⅓			5 tbsp. + 1 tsp.	16
⅜	3	6	¼ c. + 2 tbsp.	18
½	4	8		24
⅝	5	10	½ c. + 2 tbsp.	30
⅔			½ c. + 2 tbsp. + 2 tsp.	32
¾	6	12		36
⅞	7	14		42
1	8	16		48

Appendix B: Common Recipe Reductions for Preschool Cooking Experiences

Reduce your favorite recipe for preschool cooking experiences by using the following table.

REDUCING ORIGINAL AMOUNTS

Original	½ original	⅓ original	¼ original	⅙ original
1 tsp.	½ tsp.		¼ tsp.	
1½ tsp.	¾ tsp.	½ tsp.	⅜ tsp.	¼ tsp.
2 tsp.	1 tsp.		½ tsp.	
1 tbsp.	1½ tsp.	1 tsp.	¾ tsp.	½ tsp.
2 tbsp.	1 tbsp.	2 tsp.	1½ tsp.	1 tsp.
¼ c.	2 tbsp.	1 tbsp. + 1 tsp.	1 tbsp.	2 tsp.
⅓ c.	2 tbsp. + 2 tsp.		1 tbsp. + 1 tsp.	
½ c.	¼ c.	2 tbsp. + 2 tsp.	2 tbsp.	1 tbsp. + 1 tsp.
⅔ c.	⅓ c.		2 tbsp. + 2 tsp.	
¾ c.	⅜ c.	¼ c.	3 tbsp.	2 tbsp.
1 c.	½ c.	⅓ c.	¼ c.	2 tbsp. + 2 tsp.

Appendix C: Increasing Common Recipe Amounts

Most recipes in this book were designed for individual preschool portions. To increase the recipes in this book for a large group or family, follow the table to multiply measurements. An adult portion counts as two preschool portions.

Amount	Multiply by 2 (double)	Multiply by 3 (triple)	Multiply by 4	Multiply by 5
1 tsp.	2 tsp.	1 tbsp.	1 tbsp. + 1 tsp.	1 tbsp. + 2 tsp.
1½ tsp.	1 tbsp.	1 tbsp. + 1½ tsp.	2 tbsp.	2 tbsp. + 1½ tsp.
2 tsp.	1 tbsp. + 1 tsp.	2 tbsp.	2 tbsp. + 2 tsp.	3 tbsp. + 1 tsp.
1 tbsp.	2 tbsp.	3 tbsp.	4 tbsp. or ¼ c.	5 tbsp.
2 tbsp.	4 tbsp. or ¼ c.	6 tbsp. or ⅜ c.	½ c.	½ c. + 2 tbsp. or ⅝ c.
¼ c.	½ c.	¾ c.	1 c.	1¼ c.
⅓ c.	⅔ c.	1 c.	1⅓ c.	1⅔ c.
½ c.	1 c.	1½ c.	2 c.	2½ c.
⅔ c.	1⅓ c.	2 c.	2⅔ c.	3⅓ c.
¾ c.	1½ c.	2¼ c.	3 c.	3¾ c.
1 c.	2 c.	3 c.	4 c.	5 c.

Index of Units

Index